A Thousand and One Stories

of

Pericón de Cádiz

A Thousand and One Stories

of

Pericón de Cádiz

José Luis Ortiz Nuevo

Translated and annotated by

John Moore

Inverted-A Press

Licking, Missouri

INVERTED-A PRESS

A

www.inverteda.com

ISBN 978-1-61879-002-6

Library of Congress Control Number: 2012934243

Cover Design by A. Katz

Cover Illustration: J. Medina

Printed in the United States of America

10 9 8 7 6 5 4 2 1

Table of Contents

Translator's Forward vii

My Pericón xi

Introit of Thanks and Self-criticism xiii

Two Sides of Pericón xvi

Introduction 1

1. Some Facts About My Life 5

2. Stories from Cadiz – and 42

3. Where, O Death, is Thy Victory? 112

4. Animals are Really Something! 124

5. Remembering the Masters 146

Epilogue: *afición* and *cante* 166

Appendices 171

References 202

About the Author and Translator 204

Translator's Forward

It is difficult to overstate the significance of this book among Spanish *aficionados*.[1] Originally published in 1975, this was a ground-breaking work: one of the first examples of oral histories collected from flamenco artists. Several similar books followed, but this is the one that is best known and loved. In the flamenco world of the early 1970s, Juan Martínez Vílchez, (1901-1980) or "Pericón de Cádiz," was known as one of the leading exponents of *cante* in the style of Cádiz, a veteran of the by-then waning *fiesta* scene, a link to early twentieth century flamenco, and a former featured artist from *La Zambra*. But most importantly for our purposes, he was known as the epitome of a witty *Gaditano* story teller. Surely because of this reputation, José Luis Ortiz Nuevo lugged his tape recorder to Pericón's Madrid apartment, and, plying his subject with whiskey, proceeded to collect what was to become a classic in the now extensive flamencological literature. Out of print, but not forgotten, for decades, the book was re-released in 2008, when it won the prestigious DeFlamenco.com award for "best book on flamenco." In this translation I hope to bring Pericón's world to English-speaking readers through Pericón's own words (bolstered with annotations, short biographies, place descriptions, and glossary items).

It is rare to be able to enter an alien world through the eyes of one of its denizens. But this is exactly the opportunity these thousand and one stories afford us. As Ortiz Nuevo notes below, the bulk of these stories are situated in Cádiz during a twenty-year period between the late teens and the mid-thirties of the twentieth century. Hence, we are transported to the streets of a vibrant, yet desperate city in a country that was

---

1 Names, places, and italicized words may be described in the Appendices.

struggling to enter the modern world. Perhaps the over-reaching theme that unifies the thousand and one stories is *canina* – a down-on-the-heels hunger that brings to mind skeletal scavenging street dogs. A type of gallows humor is superimposed upon the daily struggle for survival and mitigates an otherwise intolerable situation. Quick-witted humor in the face of despair has always been a hallmark of Cádiz – it is the essence of its famous *gracia*.

Nowhere does Cádiz put its *gracia* on display as much as during Carnival. The descriptions found herein sparkle with music, poetry, satire, and antics, which, if transported to a contemporary university Art department, could well bolster the tenure file of an aspiring performance artist.

Other stories chronicle Pericón's experiences and terror during the onset of the Spanish Civil War, its aftermath and, again, crushing poverty and *canina*. When Nationalist forces took over the major cities of Andalucía and sought to purge Republican support, any pretext – union membership, leftist sympathies, denunciation by a disgruntled neighbor – could result in a nighttime knock at the door, arbitrary arrest, torture, and a firing squad. Because Pericón had once performed two left-leaning *fandangos* verses – not because of political conviction, but to avoid being upstaged by a kid in short pants – he hid at home and waited for the *falangistas*.

During the early 20th century, flamenco artists lived largely from the largess of *señoritos* – a class of wealthy men who ranged from petit bourgeois to idle landed gentry. They hired the company of flamencos, prostitutes, and others – sometimes out of *afición*, sometimes for show, but most often for ribald debauchery. The artists humored their egos and eccentricities, and withstood their all-nighters angling for a "good present" – whatever the *señoritos* decided to pay. Nothing was agreed on nor guaranteed. Pericón's stories contain perhaps the best published description of this dynamic

– again, with his charming wit and largely without bitterness. In the epilogue, however, he does finally voice his opinion. As the precarious existence afforded by *señoritos* waned during the difficult post-war years, Pericón followed the large internal migration from Andalucía to Madrid. There he was able to earn a better living from a larger and wealthier *señorito* class, and eventually moved out of private *fiestas* and into the emerging *tabalo* venue. These were the new flamenco nightclubs – they offered nightly performances and a steady paycheck. Through his thirteen years at *La Zambra*, Pericón finally achieved a degree of financial stability, largely due to the promotion of flamenco as a tourist attraction in the 1960s.

Ortiz Nuevo describes this book as an impressionist mural populated by Cádiz, its characters, and its *cante*. In fact this mural resembles a Felliniesque landscape: beggars, hustlers, hunchbacks, street urchins, Gypsies, prostitutes, artists, drunks, madmen, undertakers, Northern shopkeepers, the idle rich, and talking animals – all loosely held together by *cante flamenco* and the struggle to survive in a Cádiz that lived (and lives) on a hope and a joke. Two famous *bulerías* verses from Cádiz sum this up: the first celebrates a famous beggar, the second the *gracia gaditana*:

A mí me ha dicho mi prima,	My cousin told me,
la del barrio del Balón,	the one from the Balón neighborhood,
que van a poner monumento	they're putting up a monument
y encima María Bastón.	with María Bastón on top.
Con el caray, caray, caray	With caray, caray, caray
mira que de cosas que pasan en Cai,	see what things go on in Cádiz...
que ni las hambres las vamos a sentí	We won't even feel the hunger.
Mire usté que gracia tiene este país	See what *gracia* this land has.

Many thanks to José Luis Ortiz Nuevo, Luis Laplaza, Carola Moreno (Ediciones Barataria), and Aya Katz (Inverted-A Press) for their support of this project. Thanks also to Alicia Muñoz for clarifying numerous Spanish references and to Nicholas and Sonja Moore for proofreading and commenting on earlier versions. Finally, I wish to thank Pericón's son, Antonio Martínez Nieto, for bringing these stories to life for me – he followed in his father's footsteps with the *gracia* and *ángel* of his homeland. Sadly, Antonio passed away a few months before going to press. He will be sorely missed – I dedicate this translation to his memory.

My Pericón

(Prologue to the 2008 edition)
José Luis Ortiz Nuevo

Although I hate to say it, and even more write it, it has been thirty-some years plus days since those Madrid afternoons during the early 1970s when, with the frightfully heavy tape recorder, I sought him out, in order to listen, delight in, and preserve. I did this so that even today we can continue to enjoy his living company, through the paths of his fascinating natural inventiveness, to which flamenco *aficionados* rarely lend sufficient appreciation as a thing of genius. Rather, they treat it as exaggerated humor or simple lies adorned with wit. What they don't understand is what this deserved then and continues to deserve – the talent of his narrative memory that sprang from love, fear of hunger, death mocked, and the ability to laugh at everything, including his own ailments. For example, when a paralysis left his face disfigured, he told his friend Félix: "Look Félix, how funny! I got up the other day and went to the bathroom – looking in the mirror, I saw I had one eye on my forehead and the other near my mouth – aren't I the Martian!" Shortly after, Juan Martínez passed away: as uncomplicated as his name and surname, unrivaled as an epitome of a *Gaditano* – singer and *Caletero* – always inventing, always angling to fish from the sea of dreams, despite being faced with so many tempests of war, hunger, poverty, and disillusions of horror and fear. But these were never equal to his own power, his tireless will and resistance. Perhaps this was because of his covenant with the animal kingdom and with the gods of satisfaction and wisdom who were reflected in his image and in the mood apparent from the smile on his face. Or from the continual enchantment brought on by the surprising satisfactions and delights which were behind all of what is related here – now just as much, if not more so, than thirty-some years ago, plus days.

Introit of thanks and self-criticism

(Prologue to the 1975 edition)
José Luis Ortiz Nuevo

When the idea came to me to collect these tales which I offer here as the informal memoirs of Pericón de Cádiz, your servant was as *canino* as Juan Martínez was on that night when he took advantage of Smokey's canine intelligence.[2]

I had just completed my military service, and a grant from the Center for Andalucian Music and Flamenco Studies allowed me to embark on this project: to tape record the thousand and one stories that Pericón told me over two short months, digging with generous tenacity into the immense field of his years and days. Afterwards, it was necessary to transcribe his words – so well spoken and *gaditano* – into the cold receptacle of numbered notebooks. Then came the real work.

Imagine the torrent of eyes, hands, rhythm, humor, pain, good-will, and art, propelled by and contained within the testimonials of a man who, during his childhood, was captain of two hundred kids, who suffered hunger, but rose to the heights of great *cante* ...

And imagine learning of a frightening world upon which constant poverty and necessity builds monuments of its personalities that are flying objects, that are songs ...

Well, that is what I found in Juan Martínez, and from there came the exposition I offer here: of course fragmentary, of course incomplete, and of course far from what came from Pericón's mouth.

---

2 See Part 4, "Pericón Thief".

My idea then was to intervene as little as possible: record, redact, and arrange from the rich terrain of images I received. Only for the order of presentation that follows am I alone responsible.

These stories contain neither reliable dates nor flamencological facts. I think of it as a great impressionist mural, upon which plays the color of Cádiz, its people and its *cantes*, through a gestalt experience supported by a narrative thread. One which is more concerned with being able to float through time and space, than with fixing concrete dates and places.

Everything told here, except what is established as occurring earlier, could happen in any corner of Juan Martínez's life given his immediate surroundings. Except for events from other times and places, these are particular and essential aspects of Pericón's early life – a life which witnessed the *gaditano* hubbub of the coaches and the bars, of the Mellizos, and of the Espeletas. All this during approximately twenty years – from his artistic beginnings until the Civil War in '36.

The book is organized into five parts: the first presents intimate aspects, purely biographical, of the life of the singer. The second part is Cádiz: its *fiestas*, its quirks, its parties, and its characters. "Where, O Death, is thy victory", and "Animals are really something", the third and fourth parts, are also definitively and essentially Cádiz – they are separated out because of their thematic content and because they clearly stand out from the rest. The chapter about the animals stands out in particular – it is one of the most delicious adventures that Pericón's rich imagination offers. Finally, "Remembering the masters" pays a final homage to those whose works contributed to our artist's formation. And the epilogue: a simple testimonial of opinion.

That's all. Thanks to doña Rosario for her constant support in the development of this work, to Jumán for the photographs, to Rocío for her transcriptions, and to Fernando Quiñones, author of the prologue, which comes next.

Two sides of Pericón

Fernando Quiñones

Juan Martínez, "Pericón de Cádiz", differs in my memories from all the other singers I have known, dealt with, or seen. This is because he left a special mark – an unforgettable mark from my childhood, framed in an almost familial context. My father, a doctor in the Cádiz neighborhood of La Viña, had him as a patient over many years. Thus, he heard many interesting, curious, or funny references to the flamenco world from his lips. For example, knowing my father to be an enthusiast of *bel canto*, Pericón, one day, told him:

"Don Manué, don't think there is that much difference between opera and flamenco – it's just that in opera, everything goes up and in flamenco, everything goes down."

I think with this, Pericón was alluding to a concept – very personal – about the position of the voice. He was alluding to high versus low registers, but also conveying – consciously or subconsciously – with that unsolicited and unexpected explanation his own perceptions about the social status of the two genres: the high social status, the well-off means, and the high life of opera, as opposed to the humble, vulgar, and debased status of Gypsy-Andalucian folkloric arts – always with one hand out and one behind the back. This was even more so in those years of exacerbated *canina*: a term that Pericón uses frequently – a term that recalls the far-off times of *El Buscón*, *Alfarache*, and *Lázaro de Tormes* (although the classic picaresque literature doesn't use it).[3]

---

3 The picaresque novel was a genre in Spain from the 16th to 19th centuries, which celebrated the humorous exploits of characters from the

In that Cádiz of the early 40s – shining but ailing, shivering in the destitute post-war sun – Pericón, still young, but with a touch of grey at his temples and with a ducal or cardinal air, always went well-dressed and clean shaven against the elements. He paused in an almost ritual manner, but without abandoning the *ángel*, which accompanied him always, and thus impressed my childish imagination. He was a boulder, a first and legendary guidepost to a world of the popular art of Andalucía that was awakening in me a sensibility, still waiting to gel, but already intuited and loved to some degree.

My father lightly squeezed my hand before greeting the man who came down the cobblestoned street. He was dignified, wore a necktie, had his gleaming hair slicked back, and, although he didn't realize, he brought for me behind his back venerable and majestic premonitions of things divined and ancient, but still present.

"This is Pericón, the flamenco singer," my father said.

Somehow, seeing him in the wings of that announcement – between admiration and affection – it was like Alberti's poem about Haley's comet: "I was then what I hadn't been." The warmth of an *afición* began to beat in me, which would only grow with time.

I didn't hear him sing then – that would happen much later. I was seventeen or eighteen, when one night, along with the pontifical Aurelio,[4] I somehow slipped into *La Privadilla*. There - engraved for always – I received a double blow of grace and distinction, with which Pericón dressed his *cantes*. This was complemented by an impression – more rational than emotional – of the mastery, professionalism, and knowledge

lumpen class, whose quick wits were juxtaposed with a corrupt society. *Lazarillo de Tormes* (anonymous, 1554) was an early work in this genre, as was *Guzmán de Alfarache* (Mateo Alemán, 1599). Quvedo's *El Buscón* (circa 1604) is the best known such work. Many of Pericón's stories have a picaresque air to them.

4 Aurelio Sellé.

that permeated everything. I can't tell you how many times since then I've listened to Pericón sing, along with his compatriot and near contemporary, Manolo Vargas– in private parties among the illuminati, in contests, on stages, in *tablaos*, and on other occasions; be they private and intimate or resounding and emotional, such as the night of his tribute in Cádiz's Summer Theater in August of '79, or in the extensive collection of his recordings which I know, love, and possess. But none of this will ever diminish the value of his interpretations from that night in *La Privadilla* in which I remember above all his excellent technique, mastery, and execution.

José Luis Ortiz Nuevo, the *alma pater* of the now well-established and famous *Porra de Archidona*[5], and author of works and exegeses on the flamenco world, has now brought us this book about Pericón. I believe that Ortiz Nuevo, wisely employing a practice that has already borne abundant and celebrated fruit in many fields, tries to exclude his own presence as author as much as possible. Instead he depends on the luck of the tape recorder and cedes the job of populating the pages to the protagonist alone, to reflect not only on happenings, but things desired or even imagined by him and many others. In this last sense, Pericón's imagination is not of short-lived fame. It is important to clarify that for a man like the one before us, to imagine is never, or almost never, to lie. Jorge Luis Borges has suggested more than once that it is impossible to clearly distinguish realism and fantasy in literature – after all, nothing can be more fantastic, unexpected, and unimaginable than life itself. Everything that goes through

---

5 The *Festival de la Porra Flamenca* was a *cante* festival that once existed in Archidona, Ortiz Nuevo's hometown in the province of Málaga. Like the *Gazpacho de Morón* and the *Potage de Utrera*, this was a food-themed festival (*porra de Archidona* is a thick gazpacho-like dish).

our heads, our hearts, and our sensibilities forms part of life, given that it forms part of who we are. Pericón's rich, even torrential, fantasy will provide the reader with incidents and passages more or less difficult to square with the canon's reality. On the other hand, it is fallibility, as we see on a daily basis, that rules our everyday reason. One must not forget that even in the most implausible legend there is a foundation of reality, transformed by time. In the stories and memories of Pericón, what was, what could have been, and what for him is, are indistinguishably mixed. For example no one can nor should believe the story where a dog deprived of his money (!) because of the needs of a singer, reproaches the singer for his behavior "speaking in a dog's voice," and insults him. But intelligent readers would be going astray if they didn't appreciate that behind the story there was something truly experienced – a man's guilty feelings towards an animal, a surreal sequence of events, and a verification of a human episode, with a foundation of reality and tenderness. However, this is related fantastically and humorously by a popular artist, whose creative capacity and flight of imagination requires that he go – and go he does – beyond the confines of his profession.

Apart from the easy appreciation of the clear biographical and flamencological sections of the book, whoever cannot immediately connect with those other personalized nuances of the biography would do better to just put the book down and find other texts that repeat over and over that 2+2=4. The two faces of strong realism and powerful fantasy that these pages contain require – without much effort on the part of the reader – a flexible attitude of intelligent understanding that is able to discern the nature of different, changing, and sometimes complex meanings in each of the events and moments. These evidence sociological norms that correspond to a previous period, desolate and cruel, of a tragic Andalucía, drowned in crushing poverty and backwardness, even in the city of *gracia* and humorous clarity. In this sense, the truth and innocence of Pericón's testimonials offer us, through his thousand and one stories, diverse passages and monuments: some full of humor, others crude and brutal, and yet others with an arbitrary and inconceivable fabulous quality. Yet all of them a perfect reflection of a period of Andalucía for whose desperation there isn't enough room for tears.

This is the objective history of a man, of regions, and of a world and time; it is also a subjective personal history of a sincere, spirited, and credulous mentality as well as something magical: the entire extroverted landscape of a long life lived within and for Art. In some way, sociology and poetry, flamencology and narrative, truth and dreams – all these come together in these unique pages.

A Thousand and One Stories

of

PERICÓN DE CÁDIZ

xxii

INTRODUCTION

When I was in Cádiz, living from my cante, it was a rare day when I wasn't with Antonio el Mellizo looking for work. We went from bar to bar looking for *fiestas*. When one of us would get one, he'd start plugging for the other one, trying to convince them to hire him as well.

I remember one night we were in the Tres Reyes when a very pleasant man entered and began hugging Mellizo. The man was from Madrid, don Miguel Martínez, and because he was a fish exporter, they called him "Pescaíto". Boy, did this Pescaíto know about *cante*!

So, after the greetings, they went into a private room for a *fiesta*. After awhile, Antonio el Mellizo started plugging for me: "Don Miguel, I want to introduce you to a kid who I think you'll like a lot."

"Of course Antonio, whatever you want." So they called me: "Pericón, come on – I'm going to present you to don Miguel Martínez, one of the greatest experts on *cante* in all of Spain."

"No, kid – don't pay any attention to him."

But I said: "No – if Antonio says it, it's because it's true."

"OK, well let's forget about that, I'd like to hear some cante."

Antonio started singing, as only he could. When he'd sung three or four times, don Miguel said: "OK, Antonio let's hear how your godson here sings."

I knew that don Miguel liked the *soleá* of Enrique el

1

Morcilla a lot; since I could sound just like Enrique, I told Campinetti:

"Put it there for *soleá*."[1]

No sooner had I warmed up – sounding exactly like el Morcilla – when don Miguel jumped up and began to hug me.

"*Ole*! *Viva* Enrique!"

I continued singing, the *fiesta* went on, and when we finished I saw that I had made a good impression. He gave us a very good present, we said goodbye, each of us went home, and don Miguel left Cádiz – I didn't see him again for a long time.[2]

Twenty years later I came to Madrid to sing in the *fiestas* at the Villa Rosa. One night when I was there, don Miguel Martínez came in. When he entered, all the artists went crazy greeting him because he was known as a great *aficionado* who really listened to *cante*. He went to the bar and called the artists he liked for a *fiesta*.

I remember that he kept looking at me, and finally asked: "Can I buy you a drink, friend?"

"Of course, don Miguel."

"Don't I know you?"

"Yes – and I know you – I'll tell you where you know me from."

"Please do, because I'm trying to remember."

---

[1] "*Ponla ahí por soleá*." This refers to placing the capo on a certain fret that matches the key that Pericón would sing *soleá* in.

[2] The custom of giving a *regalo* or "present" was the way *señoritos* paid the artists. Nothing was agreed on beforehand, hence the artists had to try to do whatever they could to ensure a good "present" at the end of the *fiesta*. This theme is played out in many of these stories. See Mitchell (1994) for a polemical view of the psychology and sociology of the interaction between flamenco artists and *señoritos*, including discussion of several of the stories presented here.

"Well, you see, one night you came into the Tres Reyes in Cádiz and ..."

"Don't say anymore! It was a night that I was with Antonio Mellizo and he presented a kid – very pale with black hair – I called him the 'black sheep'. That was you?"

"Yes don Miguel, that was me."

"Well, let's go into the room."

In the room there was a fiesta with eight or ten artists: Mairena, Juanito Mojama, el Niño Valdepeñas, el Cogetrenes ... In other words, a bunch of us – and just him without a woman – just there to listen to cante.[3]

The *fiesta* began – one sang, then another, etc. During a break from singing, we began talking about *cante* – whether it came from the Moors, from the Gypsies, this, that, ... Finally, don Miguel said to me:

"Well Pericón, you don't have anything to add?"

I said: "Listen, don Miguel, nobody knows the origin of *cante flamenco*. But what I do know is something Enrique el Morcilla once told me. He said that when he was a boy, his father, Enrique del Mellizo, had told him about a man who had showed him a book that said:

> In 1512 there was someone who wrote musical scores for *cante flamenco*. Scores for *cante flamenco*! In one he put a *soleá*, in another a *seguiriya*, and in another a *malagueña*...

In that year – 1512 – a ship came into Cádiz. They started unloading the cargo; when they

[3] In some cases, *señoritos* would bring prostitutes to their *fiestas* (more on this below) - the idea was that it was to be a night of debauchery - wine, women, and song. The reference to the fact that no women were present underscores what a serious *aficionado* don Miguel was.

were finished, they realized that a strange bundle was left – one without any address or return address on it. They asked themselves:

"What could this be?" "What is it?" "What's this?" "Let's see ..."

So they cut it open and saw that it was full of musical scores. Scores for *cante flamenco*!

"What's this?" "Oh!" "Ah!" "*Cante Flamenco!*"

So they took the best scores out of the bundle, closed it up, and sent it to Jerez. In Jerez the same thing happened, they took some scores out, and sent it on ...

That way the bundle went on up to Sevilla, to Málaga, etc., until it was empty. But the very best scores stayed in Cádiz.

This is why in Cádiz they sing better than anywhere else in Spain. This is why the greatest interpreters have come out of Cádiz and its province: Chacón from Jerez, Los Mellizos from Cádiz, Tomás el Nitri from Puerto de Santa María, Manuel Torre from Jerez, ..., and other artists too numerous to mention that were born in Cádiz or its province.

Of course, when I finished this story, don Miguel Martínez came up, hugging me, saying:

"*OLE, VIVA CAI!!!*"[4]

---

[4] In the local dialect, Cádiz is sometimes pronounced [káj], transcribed as 'Cai', where both the final consonant and medial /d/ are elided. This pronunciation is often somewhat self-conscious, and used to underscore something typical of Cádiz - in this case, Pericón's witty story. More often, locals only elide the final consonant, yielding [káði].

4

1. SOME FACTS ABOUT MY LIFE

I, Juan Matínez Vílchez, artistically known as "Pericón de Cádiz", was born in Cádiz September 20, 1901; I was the son of Adolfo and María; I was born at number 22 Marasal Street, now called Vea Murguía.

On May 3rd – the day of the Cross of May – in 1923, I was married to Rosario Nieto Viloria, fifteen years of age.

Our first son was born on June 21, 1924, but died at six months from a bad epidemic. Our second was born on September 30, 1925; his name is Juan. On May 7, 1928 the third was born – Antonio; in 1931 our fourth came – a girl named Carmen – on October 10th. The car stopped there.

Today I'm a grandfather five times over at 73 years of age.

Follies and Hunger

When I was a little boy, things were always badly off in my house. My father worked, but because he was disabled, he didn't work much. Then there was my brother Mateo, who was always playing the fool; my poor sister María, who was lame; and my brother Ricardo, who was always playing cards. He didn't want to do anything else – he'd sit down to play *mus* from seven in the morning until eleven at night. He wouldn't stop playing all day; when he came home, his mouth and lapels would be covered with chalk, from marking scores and chain smoking. My sister Anita, of course, was the only one who looked out for us. My brother Manolo got a job in Eukera,

5

married and was on his own. Pepe worked as a waiter and was tied up with his job.

By then we had moved to Pasquín Street; there Ricardo started working at a bakery called La Cooperativa. I remember the huge iron gate where my brother would throw me bread: I'd come at nine at night and knock on the gate with one of those old iron knockers – that way my brother knew it was me. From inside he'd throw me a *cundi* or a *boba*; he'd say: "*Niñooooooo*!!!"

Then he'd throw the *cundi*; I'd run it home and then be there again knocking at the gate: "Plommm!!! Plommm!!! Plommm!!!" – another *cundi* or a *boba*. In this way I'd bring home two or three kilos of bread, because, of course, one has to eat every day, and with the salaries back then...

And did I ever eat! I ate like a file!

When I was seven or eight I went to a school run by monks that was on Corralón Street. I remember that I was worse than bad – no one could put up with me. My poor sister Anita had to pull on my ears so hard they almost came off. I didn't want to go to school, and I'd escape out of the first window I saw. My poor sister had a horrible time pulling on me to get me to go. Every day at school I was punished, and my mother had to come get me. This went on until one day I went too far and created a huge scene. It happened when one of the brothers hit me with a ruler. I picked up an inkwell and threw it at the brother – you should have seen him. The director sent for my mother and told her that if I was to continue at the school, she had to give them permission to punish me in any way they saw fit. Of course, my mother said no, and had to pull me out of that school and enroll me in another – a private one.

I don't remember if this school was on San José Street or La Torre Street. What I do remember is the teacher. This guy had at least eleven kids at home, and given what a teacher earned in those days, he had to take advantage of us to feed his children.

The school was on the ground floor – there was an adjoining patio that we played in; in the middle of the patio there was a well.

The teacher, for whatever little thing we'd do, would shout: "Pepito! What are you doing?"

"No sir, look, it's just that ..."

"Come here! I'm not going to punish you kneeling or anything like that. I'm going to do something even worse, so that you never do such things again. Give me your lunch!"

You should have seen the lunch: breaded chops, fillets, ...; since all the kids were butchers' sons. He'd take the lunch and say: "Look what I'm doing with your lunch."

And then he would take the lunch and throw it into the well.

After awhile the same with another kid's lunch, then another, until the well started to look like a grocery store.

Of course, since I was so bad, my lunch went into the well too; the two hard-boiled eggs that my poor mother had given me – into the well! Then, after we'd left for the day, the teacher pulled the bucket out of the well with all the lunches. This way his kids were all plump and we were all *caninos*.

I didn't learn to read, write, or anything in this school, nor the other one – I never paid attention to anything. They could've killed me and I wouldn't have paid attention. I was one of those impossible headstrong kids. When my poor mother realized this, she said: Forget it; let him do whatever he wants."

That's when I started going to the *Campo del Sur* with the men who played *inglés*. This was a coin toss game that was illegal. They'd draw a line on the ground – I stood at the line barefoot to show where it was and acted as judge. They would throw the *perras;* whoever's came closest to the line got to throw first. If they were playing with five coins, then they'd take the five coins in one hand, and leave seven or eight on the side:

"Heads!"

"Tails!"

"Two *pesetas* on heads!"

"One *peseta* on tails!"

"*Vaa!*"

The five coins flew through the air, and if three landed heads-up, then those whoever bet on heads won, if three came up tails ... Whoever won the bet would give me a *perra chica*; *perra* by *perra* until the game was over. Other times, since the game was illegal, they had me standing guard at the corner of Sagasta Street to watch out for cops. I remember one day a guy had won three or four bets, but hadn't given me anything. Finally I got mad and said: "Hey man, remember that I'm here on the corner!"

"I haven't won one yet."

"No – you haven't won one – you've won five!"

Then I saw two cops coming – I said to myself – "They'll see – I won't let them know." And I didn't; I just stood there at the corner and when the cops came by I said: "They're playing *inglés* over there." The cops gave them all such a beating.

That's how I spent several years – doing naughty things and being a bad kid.

I remember there was a watchman in the Cruz Verde – he was a tiny man, but one day he hit me. I got so mad that I wanted throw him into the bay. So I told two or three of my toadies: "We need to throw this guy into the water – we'll put him in a sack and throw him in."

We never actually threw him in, but if I had said "throw him in!" then, between seven or eight kids, they'd get him in the bag and take him to the waterfront.

The thing is that back then I was worse than bad. I had 200 kids at my command – 200 kids! All the kids from the neighborhood respected me as if I were actually their captain. On Pasquín Street, in a house on the corner with a long side street (the house where Silverio Franconetti gave a concert before going to America) I had installed my headquarters in a huge patio.[5] From there I commanded two or three kids to collect cigarette butts. Then another two or three would roll them into cigarettes and sell them to the water vendors – those that sold water to the houses in Cádiz. We'd sell ten or twenty cigarettes for a *perra chica*. I used the money to buy colored paper and wood to make toy sabers. That way the kids looked like a regular regiment. We trained in the Campo del Sur, until I said: "I want everyone here tomorrow at three in the afternoon. We have to take the barrio del Mentidero!"

All my kids were there, and when I said "To Mentidero!", we went with our pockets full of rocks. When the municipal police saw us, they would hide themselves in the doorways. Then I'd yell: "To the grocery stores! Don't leave a box of biscuits alive!" After the assault, I'd split up the loot with my kids – each with their share of biscuits.

Of course with kids, it's the same as with anyone – when they see one that is really bad and not scared of anything, they make him their boss. That's why they made me captain – Captain of the Kids! Nor did anyone dare rebel – even if he was older than me. If one did, I'd say: "For what you did, I'm going to smash your face in, and on top of that, this afternoon, when you come out with the *pringá*, you have to give it to me."[6]

---

[5] Franconetti's concert of would have been his last before fleeing Spain (through the port of Cádiz).

[6] The incident seems to refer to children being sent out with some of the stew meat in a sandwich for an afternoon snack. Pericón, always looking for food, seems to have learned something from that schoolmaster after all.

Then, in the afternoon: "Here's the *pringá.*"

Boy, did I ever feast on *pringá* – a piece of bread, a piece of bacon, and a piece of meat.

I went on like that leading the pack of kids for several years; they called me "Captain Pericón." That was because I wanted to be a *picador,* but with my kid's pronunciation, it came out *"picaror"* or *"pricaror".* There was a local cop on Pasquín street who couldn't understand what I said, so he gave me the nickname of Pericón: "What? You don't want to be a *picaor?* Well, then you'll be Pericón, Pericón, Pericón."

And the name stuck for my whole life. Imagine how long ago it was when Agapito the cop gave me that name. I was just a ten-year-old kid.

All the things I did to eat back then – I was always starving, and there was never enough at home.

I'd often go to the barracks and eat cans of *Gabi* until I'd burst. I'd come to the barracks and they'd throw me field rations. Then I'd eat the *Gabi.* Once, when I was really hungry, I ate two cans of *Gabi* with that red powder they put on it. I nearly died – at home I kept throwing it up, and my poor mother, not knowing about the red powder, thought I had busted a gut.

Other times I'd go through the dumpster in front of Capuchinos and wait for the garbage cart – it came with four or five boxes of rotten bananas. I'd take two or three dozen home, peel them, put them in a dish, add sugar and cinnamon, and mash them with a fork – boy, were they good! I'd stuff myself.

I also collected firewood from the docks. I would fill a bucket with wood and take it to a sweetshop on Juan de Andas Street. There they traded the wood for candy crumbs, cookie pieces, broken chocolate yolks, and anything else that was broken. They'd give me a huge paperful. Once among all the broken candies there was even a mouse nest.

I also liked to fish. On the *Cuesta de Las Calesas* there was a river next to the train tracks. I'd go with a hook and mackerel guts to fish for *coñetas* – a kind of crab called *coñeta*. I'd drag the baited line on the bottom, catch the crabs and eat them right there.

All of this went on until I got my first job. By then people knew that I sang a little, so they called me to sell candy with a *pregón*. I walked through Cádiz with the candies on a tray and sang:

¡Ay, caramelos, caramelos!	Candy! Candy!
¿Quién quiere mis caramelos?	Who wants my candy?
Los de menta llevo yo;	I have mints;
comprármelos señoritos;	buy them from me gentlemen;
comprármelos por favor...	buy them from me please ... [7]

With the voice I had then... people called me from the balconies and made me repeat the *pregón*. But they never bought my candies; they paid me as if they'd bought some, but the candies stayed in the tray. The same thing happened with the coaches: one would come by, I was called, I'd go in with the people having a *juerga* inside, I sang for them – the *pregón* and other things too, but the candy never got sold.[8] Of course, when the owner came by, I couldn't tell him about the money I had made from the *pregón* and since I didn't sell any of the candies, he fired me.

---

[7] Pericón demonstrates this *pregón* in the *Rito y Geografía del Cante Flamenco* television series.

[8] At that time in Cádiz, it was common to hire a coach and several artists to have moving *juerga*.

Into the Cante

By the time I was four or five I already could sing a few things. But I was so shy that in order to hear me, they had to put me inside a cupboard; I sang from inside as if it were a gramophone.

But later, once I started singing in earnest, all I wanted to do was sing.

By the age of nine I had overcome my shyness; every night seven or eight of us would get together on the corner of Pasquín street to sing and play *palmas*. Back then I sang a *malagueña* about *un pelo* ('a hair') that I'd heard on the gramophones: "*Aaaaaay un pelo.*" With the voice I had back then, it came out beautifully. Of course, all the women stopped to listen; others came out on their balconies; still others called for me to keep singing. It went on like that past midnight, when my mother came to take me home.

After that I began to be known on the Cádiz scene. Whenever I came outside, people called me right away to sing in the coaches. I sat up with the coachman and sang, like I said, while driving around Cádiz. From there, from the coaches, I began to rise up in the world. Since I was well-liked, people called me to go sing here and there. This went on until I was twelve and I got my first contract.

Perico Pavón, the brother of Regaera, who had heard me sing in the coaches, called me over one day and said: "Pericón, would you like to go to Puerto Real with me and sing on Saturdays and Sundays?"

Of course, since Puerto Real was so close to Cádiz, I said: "Look, wouldn't it be better to go on Saturday evening, sing that night, and then come back to Cádiz and be home. Then we can go back the next day."

"OK, fine, I'll pay you a *duro* for the two days and pay for the train."

So we worked there Saturdays and Sundays – the place was packed. The show started around eleven and went on until five or six in the morning. I got up on an impromptu platform, sang two or three things, and got down – I'd do this ten or twelve times a night. Even though I was just a kid, I already sang good *cantes*: *soleá, malagueña del Mellizo, fandangos, alegrías, bulerías...*[9]

This lasted about three months – every Saturday and Sunday singing with Perico in Puerto Real at that place that wasn't even a café or anything – just a big hall with tables and a platform without any decoration.

Then I worked the coaches and other fiestas, particularly baptisms. Since I was so wicked, I told the kids whose families were going to have baptisms that if I sang, the baby would live to be 100; but if I didn't sing, it wouldn't even last six months. The kids would tell their parents and I was called for all the baptisms.

Sometime later I worked in San Fernando at a place called Café X. They gave me the name "The king of Argentinean *cante*," even though I wasn't Argentinean at all. I got the name because I sang an Argentinean song called M*i Noche Triste* ('My Sad Night') – a kind of a *tango* – that I had made into a flamencoized version. Every night I had to sing it because the people wanted such lousy things.[10]

I also worked in Rota in a café belonging to Alonso, a

---

[9] This list demonstrates that Pericón's repertoire consists of *cante puro* 'pure flamenco', and not flamencoized popular songs (although later he mentions singing these as well).

[10] Here is a comment on popular songs (from Latin America and elsewhere) being sung in a quasi-flamenco style and being much in demand. Argentina was the source of many of these, often in the *milonga* form. A reference to a tear-jerker *milonga* is given below.

13

very good aficionado. Like in Puerto Real, I worked there Saturdays and Sundays, and like always, I tried to beg for something to take home to eat. One day it occurred to me to ask for a pumpkin. But I didn't count on what kind of person Alonso was; I asked for the pumpkin and after the show he said: "There's your pumpkin."

You should have seen it – a monster pumpkin of at least fifty kilos. Of course, since I didn't have any way of getting it home, it stayed put.

In Cádiz I also spent a period singing in a *venta* in Puerta Tierra, along the San José highway. It was in the summer; since the *venta* had a fountain for watering the mules, the owner put some boards over the trough – that's where I sat with the guitarist to sing. One night I got up a little drunk, took a wrong step, and fell headfirst into the trough. I had to sing soaking wet.

Still later, when I sang more seriously, I was offered a contract in Sevilla. I didn't want to go because I was doing well with the coaches and cafés. But a friend from Seville, don Santiago Vasallo, convinced me and found me a contract in the Olimpia de Sevilla for fifteen days. The owner paid me five *duros* and Vasallo gave me another five to sweeten the deal -- of course I went and sang for fifteen days there.

I remember that I sang a *milonga* there that made all the dance-hall girls cry. Every time I got on stage, they asked if I was going to sing their eyeliner off. The song was called *Pobre Vieja* ('Poor Old Mother'):

> *Pobre madre mía,*
> *cuántas cosas por mi bien me aconsejaba,*
> *y yo, ingrato, ni siquiera la escuchaba.*
> *Me da pena cuando pienso en lo buena que ella fue*
> *y en la escena de la tarde que el respeto le falté:*
> *con mano temblorosa el rostro me azotó,*

y luego, pensorosa, la frente me besó;
mas yo, ciego de ira, cobarde, me indigné,
y a mi vieja querida, violento, rechacé.
«Perdóname, hijo mío», se me atrevió a implorar,
«yo sé que t'he ofendío; no te pegaré más».
No me ablandó su llanto, y de casa me marché,
y a la que quise tanto, de pena la maté.
Hoy, al recordar sus penas, me jarto de llorar,
tenía razón mi vieja: no me pegará más.

My poor mother,
she counseled me on so many things for my own good,
and I, ungrateful, never even listened to her.
I am saddened when I think of how good she was
and of that afternoon when I failed to respect her:
with a trembling hand, she slapped my face,
and later, sorry, she kissed my forehead;
except I, blind with ire and cowardly, became indignant,
and violently rejected my beloved old mother.
"Forgive me, my son!" she dared to implore,
"I realize I've offended you, but I'll never hit you again."
Her pleas didn't soften me, and I stormed out of the house,
and she whom I loved so much, I caused to die of sadness.
Now, thinking of her sorrows, I cannot cry enough.
She was right, my old mother: she'll never hit me again.

Between this verse, my falsetto voice, and the things I did with it, they all cried their eyeliner off.[11]

---

[11] The reference to a falsetto voice and vocal tricks, as well as the fact that this cante is the Argentinian-inspired *milonga*, suggests that this was in a popular genre of *ópera flamenca*. While Pericón is not usually associated with this genre, it seems that he was sometimes willing to engage in it. Pohren (1988, p. 126) mentions that some of Pericón's detractors point to his participation in the *ópera flamenca* movement. While it may have been true that he sometimes followed trends that were current at the time, Pericón is much better known for solid Cádiz-style *cante*.

Falling in love

When I met my wife, she was fourteen years old: just a little girl, but with the most beautiful face I had ever seen. Of course, we fell in love right away.

I was living with one of my brothers on San Nicolás street. She came by to see a friend, a daughter of a woman my brother knew. We'd look at each other, I'd tell her things – she just a girl and me, a man of the world; but I fell head over heels in love. Finally, one day I decided to get serious.

As usual, I dressed nicely, and when she came by I asked her out for a walk. As we left, I was flattering her, and she was blushing. I took her to a sweet shop that was on Sagasta Street, on the corner of La Torre Street.[12] We got to the sweet shop and I said: "Can I buy you a sweet?"

She said "no, no," until I convinced her. We went in and I said: "Choose whichever you want."

She just stood there looking at the tray of candied pears that were thirty *céntimos* each.

"Come on, do you want a pear?"

She said "no" – they seemed so expensive...

"Don't be silly – take a pear."

She took one and ate it; we left and started chatting. Then I asked: "Would you like a beer?"

Again, she said "no, no"... so I bought her a coffee; with the coffee we talked some more about this and that, about *cante*, how she loved *cante* – and right there I sang her two or three *fandanguillos*, and then took her home.

After that, whenever she had time, she came looking for me. When I was finished with the fiestas at six in the morning, I'd wait for her. She would come with her buckets for water –

---

[12] Sagasta and La Torre are parallel streets and do not intersect.

because of course, she had told her mother she was going for water – her mother didn't want a singer – not even in a painting! We'd go down by Capuchinos and spend hours filling the buckets.

But this is true love: One night we were taking a walk – it had just rained, and there was a big puddle that stretched from Capuchinos to the bullring. Were we in love or what? Without realizing it, we walked through the puddle, hugging and kissing, all the way through the puddle – over half a kilometer, until we came to the cathedral. From there, covered with mud we continued down San Juan de Dios street.

On tour with Marchena

During the pre-war years, Marchena was an idol.[13] When we arrived in a town, the car would stop at the gate; he'd get out with one of his girls, and Antonio el Mellizo and me at his side. The four of us walked into town. As soon as we passed the first house, people started saying:
"That's Pepe Marchena."
"Look! Pepe Marchena!"
"It's Marchena."
People started following us; by the time we got to the town square, there wasn't room for everyone. What a case! I've never seen that happen with any other artist.

Of course, someone of the age of Marchena back then, with that beautiful hair and expensive clothes ... Then when he sang, with that beautiful voice and his vocal tricks ... There were people who sang better and more flamenco, but the people had made him the idol of all Spain and followed him.

---

[13] The contrast between Marchena's popularized style and pure flamenco is played out in this story.

Since he was an idol, he made sure that everything he did he did well: Once, when he didn't feel much like singing, he came on stage, sang three *fandangos*, and left the stage. You should have seen the people calling him back – the impresario was worried – Marchena wouldn't come out. Finally, he had an idea and came back: "Dear public, I'm afraid I should not be singing today because I am very sick – see, I've brought my doctor with me."

With that, he pulled Mellizo out of the wings – poor Antonio, an old man with his glasses and cane; he took Marchena's pulse right there on stage – the people gave him such an ovation! Those were the quirks of Marchena.

On that tour we worked all over: in the provinces of Huelva, Sevilla, Málaga, Córdoba ... But whenever the show was over, the torture began: Marchena would disappear, leaving us stranded in the bullring or theater. He'd finally show up at five in the morning – the quirks of Marchena.

Of course, we were all angry, I was too, naturally. Finally, one day in Sevilla, I had words with him:

"Listen Pepe, I've going back to Cádiz."

"What do you mean? We have to work tomorrow."

"Well, I'm leaving."

So I left. I took a taxi and returned to Cádiz; when I got there, everyone was saying:

"He's come back because he had a fight with Marchena." Because of this, the commissioner don Manuel López Alquín called me in: "What happened between you and Marchena?"

"Well, you see don Manuel, this, this, and this ..." And I told him everything.

"OK Pericón, but when he comes to Cádiz you'll have to work with him. First, because you're in Cádiz, and second, because if you don't, they'll take your license away. Don't be silly and at least work when you are here."

"OK, I'll do that."

Since that was the last show with him anyway, I decided to do it.

On the day of the show, I was supposed to sing after Niño Barbate. But as I was getting ready, the announcer came and told me: "No, Pericón, Marchena is going to sing now." Of course, since the people ate him up – who would dare go on after him? Exactly as planned, they ate him up – one song after another, with me having to go on next. The announcer came again and said: "Your turn."

"I'm coming."

I went out, took the microphone and said to myself: "I'm going to put it all on the line."

Then I said: "Dear public, dear public, since I'm in my own town, and until now, no one has sung real flamenco, I'm going to sing *soleá*, I'm going to sing *siguiriyas*, I'm going to sing *malagueñas del Mellizo*; then I'll sing *alegrías*, and then whatever you ask me to, because I'm in no hurry."

The people ate me up too. God gave me that moment of inspiration and my voice was in great form. That was one of my greatest times singing to an audience – the night I sang in the bullring in Cádiz after Marchena.

The contest at Price

In 1936 they organized a cante flamenco contest at the Circo Price in Madrid. They sent announcements everywhere saying that they would pay the expenses for anyone who competed. I decided to sign up – with me two others: El Troni and Chiclanita. The three of us signed up for *soleá* and *siguiriyas*. There were three prizes: a 1,000 *peseta* one for *soleá* and *siguiriyas*, a 750 *peseta* prize for *malagueñas* and *tarantas*, and then a 500 *peseta* prize for *fandangos* and other easier *cantes*.

So we went to Madrid to compete. You should've seen

the number of singers! At least 140 artists and *aficionados*. Of course, they had to hire enough guitarists to go around, so they hired two or three from Madrid and another two or three from Sevilla – all very good.

During the three days of the contest, whenever you went into the theater there would be *cante flamenco*. If you went there at seven in the morning – *cante flamenco;* if you went at two in the morning – *cante flamenco*. One after the other: one singing *fandangos*, another singing *fandangos* ... Even though *fandangos* was all the rage then, it was just too much *fandangos*. So, when it was my turn – I was number 96 or 97 – I decided to sing *soleá* and see what happened.

But no sooner had they announced me, than everyone in the theater was saying: "Oh – from *Cádis!*" "*Cádis!*" "Pericón de *Cádis?*" "Let's see - *Cádis!*" "Oh, from *Cádis!*" [14]

There I was, under a spotlight that gave a hellish heat, putting up with all of that... So I stood up and raised my hands for people to be quiet, but they wouldn't be quiet, and kept shouting "*Cádis*". But little by little they calmed down; when they were done, I said:

"Ladies and gentlemen! I, being from Cádiz, have noticed that so far no one has sung real *macho cantes*. And I, being from Cádiz, am going to sing *macho cantes* for you."

So I started singing soleá – you should have seen how I stirred them up! I sang three *soleares* from Cádiz. I finished and they gave me such an ovation. Then I sang *siguiriyas* – three different styles of *siguiriyas* – you should have seen the reaction. Then, since I could sing whatever I wanted, I sang *alegrías* – and that was the clincher. The audience went crazy – the whole theater on their feet – I thought they'd bring the

---

[14] The spelling '*Cádis*' in the original suggests an effeminate pronunciation, based on the common perception that Cádiz has a large Gay population. See Part 2, "La Zubiela".

house down. The three days I spent singing *soleá* and *siguiriyas* first, then *alegrías* and *fandangos*. They gave me the first prize for *soleá* and *siguiriyas*, but I didn't see anything of the 1,000 *pesetas*. The organizer, Monserrat, came by and said: "Listen, Pericón, you've won first prize, but I can't give you the money now – you can't imagine the expenses that I've had putting this on – so many artists, train fares, food, lodgings ... Anyway, what I'll do is present you with an envelope in front of the audience, as if there were 1,000 *pesetas* inside. I give it to you; you say 'thank you,' showing it to the audience, then tomorrow, without fail, I'll give you the money in Sevilla."

So I did what he said; he gave me the empty envelope, I took it, and then took the bus to Sevilla. When I got there, he came by and said: "Listen, Pericón, I forgot that today is the second of May."

"So what's with the second of May?"

"I won't be able to pay you today because the banks are closed. But don't worry – I'll send you the money in Cádiz. Here – take this train fare, and I'll send you the money without fail."

By then I had already signed a contract for forty performances with him, at 20 *duros* a shot. This was with a troupe that he had put together of the contest winners. So he had me – I couldn't do anything. I went to Cádiz to wait for the 1,000 pesetas. Day after day went by until a received a telegram fifteen days later:

"Take the first bus to Sanlúcar tonight – we start tonight in Sanlúcar."

I'm wondering what to do – of course, I had a contract for forty shows ... So I decided to go to Sanlúcar. There Monserrat was waiting for me at a café.

"Hey, Pericón – sorry – I wasn't able to pay you that money, but don't worry – we're starting the tour, and I'll pay you the prize money."

We worked that night in Sanlúcar and he paid my salary. The next day we performed nearby; there wasn't much audience, so he paid me half. That was the way it went – one place the whole salary, another less, but no mention of the 1,000 *pesetas*. We went to Sevilla and performed in the bullring – you should have seen how much money they made, with the plaza full of people. But still no mention of the 1,000 pesetas. Finally I got fed up and told him I wouldn't go on – I didn't – I went to one of those courts they had back then and explained what had happened. They told me not to worry – that nothing would happen if I didn't finish the contract, and furthermore, he had to pay me the 1,000 *pesetas*, as well as my entire salary.

But after two or three days in Sevilla, I saw some troop movements and other things, and I thought "My God! What's going on?" I was terrified, and rushed to the train station; I got on the nine o'clock train for Cádiz and didn't get off until I had arrived there.

All because of those two verses

During the contest at the Price there was a kid from Sevilla called 'Chiquito Triana'. This kid, with his short pants and his child's voice, was such a big hit that they gave him an honorary prize. Then the troupe was formed from the prize winners and we started touring. However, nobody wanted to go on after the kid, since he was such a hit. He'd go out in his short pants and sing this verse:

Yo soy huérfano de pare,	I'm an orphan without a father,
de mare también lo soy;	and without a mother as well,
yo no tengo más calor	the only love I have
que la que tú quieras darme.	Is that which you choose to give me.
No m'abandones, agüelita, por Dios.	My God, Granny, don't leave me.

Of course, this created such a stir! The public ate it up, and the poor guy who went on next received about six handclaps. That's why no one wanted to go on after him, because it would be a fiasco – not even Canalejas, who was the star, dared go on after the kid. So they had to put him on last.

Because of this, we were all searching for something to give us some appeal to the public, when a man from Jerez came and said to me: "If you really want applause, sing these verses – you'll see how the public will love it.[15]

They were just two verses – not political or anything – just silly things. But since we were in those times, any little thing would get people stirred up. So, when it was my turn to sing after the kid, I tried out those verses – without being political or anything, never having belonged to a party ... But you should have seen the reaction: it brought the house down.

It continued that way until I returned to Cádiz over the 1,000 pesetas. I was in Cádiz when the Civil War started. Seeing all the horrible things that went on, I was terrified about having sung those verses, so I didn't leave the house.

My wife, children, and I were left without any money – all because of those two verses. I had to sign the family up for charity so that we'd at least get some food and clothes.

All of this even though I had never been political nor

---

[15] Antonio Martínez Nieto, Pericón's son, provided one of these verses, which Pericón sang as a *fandangos*.

A caballo en su silla,	Sitting on horseback,
va un caballero.	Goes the gentleman.
Atrás va un pobre obrero	Behind goes the poor worker
con fango hasta las rodillas,	up to his knees in mud,
el que le gana el dinero.	the one who earns the money for him.

belonged to anything – terrified and stuck at home – all because of those two verses ... Then one night around one or two in the morning we heard a knock at the door downstairs. My wife came out and said: "Oh, Juan! It's the *Falange*!"

There was the night watchman with the head of the *Falange* and two other *falangistas*.[16] I hid under the bed; they kept banging on the door – the doorman came out: "Who is it?"

"Listen, does Juan Martínez live here?"

I was dying – under the bed listening to all of this. They were let in; I heard their footsteps on the stairs, and then the knocking on our door. I was terrified, as was my wife, but she opened the door.

"Hello Ma'am, does Juan Martínez live here?"

"Yes, he lives here..."

"Well look, since today is Three King's Day, we've brought some clothes from charity."

My poor wife was crying with the charity clothes: "Come on out Juan, they didn't come for you; they came to bring clothes for our Juanito."

It made me so happy ...

Around that time in Cádiz I used to go out with a commander – he was the only one I'd go to *fiestas* with, because with him, of course, I didn't have to worry about those two verses.

We'd go to the Petí Kursal, and he would always complain about his pain from the wounds he had received at the front – but it was a lie, since he'd never been to the front. I'd play along, joking; when he started with his wounds and

---

[16] Antonio, Pericón's son, told me a different version – or perhaps a precursor to the present story. According to Antonio, the *falangistas* came looking for Pericón, indeed to arrest him. The night watchman, being a family friend, told them that Pericón had lived there, but had gone to Mexico. Only through the intervention of local *señoritos* was Pericón eventually spared.

pains, I'd ask for twenty *duros* for gauze. Of course he didn't need any gauze, and I'd keep the twenty *duros*.

One night he was at the bar pretty drunk. There were two others nearby, and pretty soon he began to insult them: this, that, and the other thing ... Finally, one of them came over and said: "Listen, I've been to the front more than you because you've never been there."

"Me? Why you!"

Of course, the guy came at him; he threw him to the floor and started a ruckus. A patrol came by and arrested him, taking him to the prison in Santa Catalina castle.

This would have been around Holy Week; my friend, stuck in jail, remembered me and wanted me to sing him some *saetas*, so he sent a soldier to get me.

I was still worrying about those two verses when I heard at around two in the morning: "Pericón, Pericón!"

I died – "they've finally come for me." I looked out over the balcony and saw a soldier and was convinced that they had come for me. They opened the door, the soldier climbed the stairs. I was trying to get dressed the best I could: a jacket with a safety pin, a pair of espadrilles, "whatever" I told myself.

The soldier arrived, my wife opened the door, and he said: "I've come for Pericón."

I left with him trembling; just to say something, I asked where we were going.

"To Santa Catalina castle."

Of course, I had heard of terrible things happening there and I realized what was in store for me – all because of those two verses ... We got to the castle, the watchman opened the doors; an ensign came out and asked: "Are you Pericón?"

"Yes sir."

"Come with me."

I went with him to the commander's cell. When I saw

him there – saw him there waiting for me, and that nothing bad was going to happen – it made me so happy that I started crying. He was crying too, the two of us hugging each other, until he said: "Godson," (he always called me that) "I've sent for you so that you can sing me a few *saetas* – since it's Holy Week, I want you to sing me some *saetas*."

"Whatever you want, Godfather."

So I sat down on the cot and sang him three or four *saetas*. He asked after my children; I told him about the charity and everything that was going on ... He lifted up the mattress and gave me ten twenty-*duro* notes to buy food for the kids with. I was stunned! I didn't know where to put them! I was crying, hugging him, thanking him, kissing him like I've never kissed anyone!

Later, a soldier took me home; when my wife saw that nothing had happened to me, and on top of that, the ten bills ... you should have seen how she hugged me.

Las Calles de Cádiz

After the war they called me to do *Las Calles de Cádiz*. I spent the next five years touring Spain with it. This show had been done before, which was when they had Ignacio Espeleta playing the role of the shoemaker. This time I played that role.

La Argentinita had rights to the production, but Conchita Piquer asked permission to re-stage it. She contacted a number of great artists: Pastora Pavón and her husband, Pepe Pinto, La Macarrona, La Malena, La Ignacia, La Albaicín and her husband, Mari Paz, Luis el Compare, Pepe el Limpio, Paulito, Rafael Ortega, Caracolillo, Josele, Melchor de Marchena, El Niño Ricardo …a pretty good line-up.[17]

---

[17] Essentially a who's who of flamenco from that period, including a number of old-timers brought out of retirement.

The show was based on true events in the barrio Santa María: There was a shoemaker there who sang very well; when the artists got out of their *fiestas* in the early morning, they would stop off at the shoemaker's house:

"*Maestro*, how are you?"

"Pretty good – have a seat, and we'll talk."

"Well, here I am – I've just come from a *fiesta*, and before going home I wanted to say hello."

"Well, let's have a *media botellita*."

And there, in the shoemaker's shop with a half-bottle, the guitarist took out the guitar, played a little, the shoemaker got excited and started to sing, the neighborhood *Gitanos* came by and played *palmas* and danced, and a *juerga* got underway ...

This is exactly what was scripted in *Las Calles de Cádiz*: I was seated on stage as the shoemaker, dressed like a shoemaker. As the curtain went up, Pepe Pinto, with a wig like little kid hair, came on singing *fandangos*. When the curtain was up, I started singing tangos de Cádiz, the one about the Plaza de la Catedral:[18]

Plaza de la Catedral	The Plaza of the Cathedral
es un verdadero encanto,	is really enchanting
porque se remea mucho	because it reminds one of
a Melilla con sus campos:	Melilla and its lands:
tiene su zoco y mezquita,	it has its plaza and mosque,
infiniá de palmeras,	endless palm trees,

[18] This satirical tango began as a Carnival *tanguillo* and is attributed to the famous *murgista* El Tío de la Tiza. Originally the last line was "*en vez de Silos Moreno, a Maimón Mójetar*", 'instead of Silos Moreno, Maimón Mójetar'. Maimón Mójetar was a Rif leader who fought the Spanish in the Rif War of 1893, when Berber forces laid siege to the Spanish Moroccan city of Melilla. The *tanguillo* is listed as having been performed by the *comparsa Los Viejos Cooperativos*, usually with a date of 1889; however, given that the Rif war would have been long over by then, the alternative 1884 is more likely. I have not heard this sung as a *tanguillo*, but is often sung as a Cádiz style *bulerías*, recorded by, among others, Manolo Vargas (on D-6) and Chano Lobato (D-9). See Discography.

y con tiempo tendrá	and pretty soon it will have
catorce o quince chumberas;	fourteen or fifteen prickly pear bushes;
y para más semejanza	and to be even more similar
debían de colocar,	they should have put,
en vez de Silos Moreno,	instead of Silos Moreno,
la cabeza del sultán.	the bust of the Sultan. [19]

Then the kid Josele came out, teasing, and trying to steal things from the table while I sang. Next to me were Melchor de Marchena and Niño Ricardo playing guitar with amazing *compás*, and the kid, with even better *compás,* coming over to me. I got up as if to hit him with my shoe mold, still singing. Right when I was about to get him, La Macarrona came on stage, in the same rhythm, playing the role of the kid's mother. She grabbed him by the scruff of the neck and took him home – me still singing – she spanking his butt exactly in *compás* with the *cante* and the *baile*, until we brought the house down.

Then La Niña de los Peines came on with a basket of flowers, singing a *pregón* though the streets of the *barrio*. It was worked out that just when the *pregón* was finished, she turned into a street and went offstage. Another ovation, because, of course, her *pregón* was beautiful.

Then Pepe el Limpio came out, dressed as an old-fashioned policeman with a saber and hat. He was after the kids that were bothering me – he asked me where they were and went off after them. Then Rafael Ortega came out playing an English tourist, also looking for the kids. Everything was framed with this wonderful *compás* that everyone had.

---

[19] The reference to *zoco* 'plaza' and *mezquita* 'mosque' is probably a play on the plaza surrounding the cathedral and the minaret-like towers, but also because there were bars in the plaza named El Zoco and La Mezquita; see Part 2, "El Vivillo". Fray Domingo de Silos Moreno was the Bishop of Cádiz, who, in 1838, oversaw the completion of the cathedral; his statue was once in front of the cathedral, but because it was often the target of desecration during the Second Republic, the Nationalists moved it to a less prominent position in 1936. It now stands next to the cathedral.

Finally, the whole *cuadro* came out doing *alegrías*. I sang: "*A Cádiz no le llaman Cádiz, que le llaman relicario* ..." ('They don't call Cádiz Cádiz, they call it the reliquary'). All the dancers came out in *compás* – to hear it was to die. First La Macarrona, then La Malena, La Ignacia, La Albaicín, Mari Paz, and finally Conchita Piquer, closing the *cuadro*. After all of this was finished, the artists came out alone: Mari Paz did her number, looking just like a doll; El Albaicín and his wife, and others as well, until finally, Conchita Piquer came out to sing her *cuplés*: *La Parrala* and *A la Lima y al Limón*.

Then finally – the last of it all – was a Christmas Eve in Jerez: all the artists came on stage with tambourines and *zambombas*, worshipping the baby Jesus and singing.[20] La Niña de los Peines sang on stage, and I answered her from the wings.

In this way we spent some good years touring Spain with *Las Calles de Cádiz*, playing to full houses wherever we went.

I remember a funny thing that happened on the road: since the trains back then were pretty bad and were always packed, so we had to earn our seats. We went straight to a compartment, and right off, Luis el Compadre or someone started telling a tale about how I had been bitten by a dog and they were taking me to the doctor. Then I pretended to have a fit – we had the compartment to ourselves within five minutes.

Cádiz, Cádiz

When *Las Calles de Cádiz* finished its Spanish tour, Conchita Piquer wanted to take the show to Argentina. I didn't want to

---

[20] Jerez is famous for its Gypsy Christmas Eve celebrations. Flamenco Christmas carols, called *villancicos*, are sung, accompanied by guitar, tambourine and *zambomba*.

go abroad, so I returned to Cádiz to stay.

In Cádiz, the situation was getting worse: fewer *fiestas,* less money, more problems ...

I knew a coal vendor who would help me out. His name was José; he had a coal store on La Palma Street, which was where I went when I was completely broke. This José loved *cante* and playing *mus* so much that whenever I was a few days without work, I had to visit him. I knew that he'd warm up with a few glasses of wine, so when it was time for him to knock off work, I went in for the kill: "How's it going, don José? Good Morning."

"Hey, Pericón – what's up?"

"Not much, I'm coming from a *fiesta* (a lie), and I just came by to say hello. Do you want to play some *mus*?"

"Sure."

By now I was working. We'd play three or four hands, each with its corresponding wine, until I saw he was ready: "Well, José, I'm going to take off."

"Wait – I want to buy you a drink at *La Habana.*"

We'd go to La Habana, ordered a *media botellita* at the bar – he didn't mind spending 500-600 *pesetas.* Then we'd go into a room – more wine and *cante* until six or seven in the afternoon. He'd pay me, and that way I'd keep things going. I hate to tell you the number of times that I had to go looking for José the coal vendor ...

When I didn't do that, I'd have to sing in the coaches, singing here and there: in the streets, in the country, on the beach ... no problem if the weather was good, but sometimes you'd get one of those winds from the East and the high surf, the coach driving down by Campo del Sur and me singing ... Finally, when we'd get to a *venta*, nobody wanted to go to a room. All they wanted to do was drink wine at the bar, and have us sing standing up, have the guitarist play standing up with his foot on a chair – in other words, a real pain.

The reason for this was that people just wanted to be seen in a *juerga*; they didn't care about *cante*. They just wanted to be seen riding in coaches or standing at the bar drinking wine and spending money.

That's how Cádiz was, but I never wanted to leave.

The Explosion of San Severiano

Three years before I went to Madrid, something happened in Cádiz that I'll never forget: the explosion of San Severiano. I remember that that night I was in La Privaílla playing *mus*; I was partnering Antonio Delgado Soto – we played against a nephew of Antonio and Sebastián, the owner of the hotel Manolita.

It was 9:50 PM, and all was fine, but suddenly the floor began shaking, the tables flying, and the chairs spinning.

"My God, what's that?!"

I ran outside and saw that the sky was all lit up: red, red, and there were pieces of burning iron ...

"Is this the end of the world?"

It looked like the sky had split open and the comets and stars were falling.

All Cádiz was dark, with cries from all over:

"Ay, my Mommy!"

"Ay, my son!"

"Ay, my Daddy!"

"My children!"

Of course, I ran out looking after my own family. I ran down Ancha Street, looking for my son Juan, who worked at a photo mart. When I got there, the poor guy was so scared he didn't want to come out. I fetched him, and then the two of us went down San José Street in the dark, stepping on broken glass, hearing cries, until we got home – we lived on Consolación Street. We found my wife and other kids there, all

31

trembling. We went inside and listened to the cries from the street. After about an hour, a military patrol passed by with a loudspeaker:

"Everyone evacuate the buildings! Everyone evacuate the buildings! There may be a second explosion!"

So we all rushed out, looking for a safe place. We finally found a tree in the middle of Corralón Street – we hid out there. Everyone was running around – some towards La Caleta, other towards the beach, others to other remote places, all waiting for the second explosion – this could have been the end of the world.

All of this without knowing what it was. Everyone had a different story: a bomb from the war, an oil tank, this, that, the other thing ... Finally we found out that it was an explosion in the torpedo stockpile in the neighborhood of San Severiano; of course, the neighborhood was leveled.

While we waited for the next explosion, which, thank God, never came, an engineer got Navy volunteers to disarm the bombs. Then, at four in the morning, the soldiers came back and said we could go home – the danger was over.

That was the most horrible thing I've ever seen; no matter what anyone says, nobody who wasn't there in Cádiz could understand what it was like. It would have been worse if the sea walls at Puerta Tierra hadn't been strong enough to withstand the wave, sending it up to the stars.

The next day, after I'd found out what had happened, I made up the following verses about the incident – later I recorded them.

No encuentro comparación　　Nothing can compare
con las murallas de Cai,　　with the sea walls of Cádiz
no encuentro comparación;　　nothing can compare;
si no hubiera sio por ellas,　　if not for them,
hubiéramos muerto to'.　　we would have all died.
Las bombas qu'explotaron　　The bombs that exploded

en los torpedos,
al llegar a las murallas,
las mandó al cielo.

No se borra de mi mente
el dieciocho de agosto,
No se borra de mi mente,
por una explosión que hubo
murieron muchos inocientes.
Cuando miré pa'l cielo
me horroricé,
porque hasta las estrellas
las ví correr.

from the torpedos,
arriving to the walls,
were sent to the sky.

I'll never forget
August eighteenth,
I'll never forget,
because of an explosión
many innocent people died.
When I looked to the sky
I was horrified,
because even the stars
I saw them fall.

This was my impression of seeing the sky burning. After that, the explosion was all anyone talked about in Cádiz. Everyone had their story. Antonio from La Privaílla had a candle in a bottle for when the lights went out. When the shock wave came, the neck of the bottle was bent so it faced downwards. In the Melus' house the curtains were cut off, as if with scissors. There were two sailors outside the door where the explosion took place: one was left stuck to the wall like a cigarette paper, the other was untouched. A kid was picked up off the street and flew off turning somersaults until he landed in the bullring. He was still alive, but the shock wave had left him naked. A man was crossing the bridge by San Severiano with his donkey; the donkey had its head severed, but the man was fine ...

People told thousands of stories. But exactly ten days later – August 28, 1947 – one man put a stop to all of it. On that day a bull killed Manolete; after that nobody remembered the explosion and could only talk about Manolete:

"A bull killed Manolete."
"A bull got Manolete and killed him."
"A bull got Manolete."
"A bull got Manolete and killed him."

"Manolete ..."

" A bull ..."

The rest was erased – that's the way of life.

Madrid, Madrid

In 1950 things were so bad in Cádiz that I decided to move to Madrid. I went up there without knowing anyone. I started asking around and found out that Manolo de Badajoz was boss. So, I went to see him and tell him my story. The guy treated me splendidly.

My first break came when a gentleman from Cádiz came to Madrid. He was the brother of don Gaspar Núñez Limón – tall and dark, with a mole on his face – very nice. When he found out that I was from Cádiz, he asked me to sing for him. I called Manolo to accompany me. That was how he saw how I behaved at *fiestas*; Manolo liked my singing and there began our friendship.

Of course, since he got the best work in Madrid, he had a *fiesta* almost every night. Whenever he could, he'd call me – that way I began to know the scene. People got to know me; whenever they asked for me, I would tell them to call Manolo because I liked his playing and was grateful for how he had opened doors for me.

That way we became good friends. Often, before going to the Villa Rosa, we got together at the Café Riego – Manolo, Montoya, and me – to talk about *cante*. I'd tell them stories from Cádiz and they'd die laughing ... then around eleven we'd go to Villa Rosa. [21]

---

[21] 'Montoya' must be a reference to Ramón Montoya. However, Montoya's death in 1949 would suggest that Pericón could not have worked with him in 1950. Pericón would have probably worked with him in Cádiz or Seville, or, perhaps, in Madrid prior to 1950.

Villa Rosa had Madrid's best. Every night there were 20-30 artists: guitarists, dancers, and singers. Upon arriving, they'd sit at their tables drinking coffee and waiting for the *señoritos*. Of course, the owner wanted a lot of artists – that way word got out that whoever wanted to hear *cante* or see *baile* had to go to Villa Rosa. Even though some took the artists elsewhere, most would stay there in a room. They would drink a *media botellita* at the bar, call this one and that, go into a room, and then do what they wanted: some would leave at two or three in the morning, some at four, and some stayed two or three days. I remember that many times Perico el del Lunar, since he knew the ropes, came in during the morning to look for stragglers. He drank his morning coffee, waited for someone to come out of a room – he got them to let him in – play for two *cantes*, and end up getting paid the same as the rest of us, who had been there all night.

In all, that time at the Villa Rosa was wonderful. They opened a second Villa Rosa in Ciudad Lineal, with the same owner, don Tomás Pajeras. This one was in a building that had been a *marqués'* palace. During the Civil War, La Pasionara had used it as her headquarters. Afterwards, the *marqués* didn't want it, so don Tomás made it into another Villa Rosa.

You should have seen it – this guy brought in the very best artists in the world, earning lots of money. Of course, since I wanted in on it too, I got Manolo to help me again. One night we went to a *fiesta* there with a *marqués*; Manolo came out to invite don Tomás in so he could see me. He liked my way of working in a *juerga*, and after a few days, called and said that if I wanted to work there, he'd tell me when – of course, the only ones who worked there were by invitation. I was thrilled, because the *fiestas* there were great. What I did was do a first pass in the old one, in Santa Ana; if nothing turned up, I'd go out to Ciudad Lineal. That way, along with my way of being, my stories, and my *cante*, things opened up for me.

From Zambra to the World

Perico el del Lunar also hung out at the Villa Rosa. He started to tell me about a *tablao* that was going to open, that would pay a regular salary, this, that, the other, and "don't be stupid" – he convinced me. So, I went to talk to the owner; he said: "OK, I'll give you a fifteen day contract."

"Come on – fifteen days? At least make it a month."

So he made it a month – and I worked there for thirteen years without missing a day.

This Zambra was the first modern *tablao* that opened in Madrid. It had a great line-up of artists. It wasn't like the Villa Rosa – instead it had a small stage. First the large *cuadro* came out, made up of twenty artists – dancers, singers, and guitarists. They performed from 11:00 to 1:00 in the morning. Then we came out with Rosita Durán. We were Perico el del Lunar, Juanito Varea, Rafael Romero, Jarrito (Montoya) – who was there sometimes, Manolo Vargas, Menese, and Enriquito Morente – the last to join the *cuadro*. Later, Perico's son, Perico el del Lunar Jr., took his father's place. I was also there, of course.

This *cuadro* was based on good *cante* – *soleá, siguiriyas, la caña* – all quality flamenco. Rosita's dances were also great; she danced *la petenera* – sometimes Rafael sang, sometime Jarrito, and sometimes me. She also danced *siguiriyas* and *caracoles*, which I also sang for. We were on stage for about an hour, followed by the large *cuadro* which closed the show. This way, for 200-300 *pesetas*, you could see all those artists. People got used to this format and began to forget about *fiestas* – in a *fiesta* it cost more just to say "good evening." Nevertheless, some still enjoyed *fiestas* and we got some great ones working at La Zambra. *Aficionados* came to listen to us, drink a few whiskies, warm up, and when we were done, they'd wait for us at the bar. Of course, when people want more *cante*: "Let's go to this or that *venta*."

We went and stayed out until the morning.

In these *fiestas* I earned lots of great tips because we had a lot of foreigners – I put on my commercial smile and brought in the dollars.

Later we did some great tours outside Spain: we worked in the Spanish Pavilion at the international exposition in Brussels, a tour of Holland, and a month-long theater engagement in London where Manolo Vargas and I made the first British flamenco recording *Flamencos Gaditanos*.[22] We also went to Rome, to the Theater of Nations in Paris, and to New York – except I stayed in Madrid for this last trip because of what happened on the way back from Rome.

We worked in a theater in Rome; on the last night, an exiled *marquesa* invited us to a party. As I recall, she just called the theater, and after settling with Casares, the owner of La Zambra, I got a cab that dropped me off at the castle. You should have seen the castle – nine floors – and me all alone climbing those huge staircases. On each landing there was a table with a statue of a naked guy, with all his parts showing and everything! I kept on climbing until I got to the party. By the time I got there everyone was already drunk – Manuela la de Ronda had tied one on, as had this one, the other one ... Probably it was because the *marquesa* had put out a tray of bonbons the size of apples that were filled with anise. If you ate six or seven of them, you were three sheets. Anyway, the party went on, it ended, the *marquesa* paid us – very well; we headed back to the pension to pack because our flight left in the morning.

But there was a huge storm brewing – horrible! We

---

[22] The Brussels exposition would have been the first post-war international exposition in 1958.

were all shaking over the thought of flying in the storm: "My God, let's see if this passes through!" No way – by the time of the flight the sky was still churning. We didn't want to board: "no – no way!" But the owner said there was no alternative – we had to board. It was like an earthquake; the plane pitched this way, then that; we were shitting ourselves – all of us dying – except Rafael Romero, who had drunk eight or ten whiskies before getting on and once strapped in, was out cold. What a trip! Instead of taking three hours, it took five and a half. When we got to Madrid I said, "This is the last time I'm getting on a plane!"

So when the time came to go to the International Exposition in New York – after getting them to raise the pay two or three times – I stayed put. I wasn't going to get on a plane again and I didn't. [23] I stayed in Madrid; when Casares saw that there was no changing my mind, he left me in charge of the artists at La Zambra while the rest worked at the Spanish Pavilion making really, really good money. They could have paid me millions and I wouldn't have gone and I didn't.

So I called Manolo de Huelva and asked him to come play for me. He didn't want to, but I finally convinced him on the condition that he play only for me. He worked out a good deal with the owner, and between the two of us and a girl who danced beautifully, we pulled through. This girl was María Angélica – while she was at La Zambra, the public loved her. She put together *la caña*, a *siguiriya*, and a *tanguillo de Cádiz*. I sang and Manolo de Huelva and Paco de la Isla played guitar.

Until they all came back from New York with their money and all went on as before.

I went on like this without missing a day, until I developed a pharyngitis that kept getting worse. So, I did my

---

[23] This was the 1964 Expo, where the flamenco performances at the Spanish Pavilion featured some of the finest flamenco.

paperwork and retired.

The Anthology

While we were at La Zambra, a group of Frenchmen came to record the first anthology of *cante flamenco*.[24] They discussed it with Perico el del Lunar and he took charge of bringing together the artists – each would sing their special *cantes*: Pepe el de la Matrona, Niño Almadén, Rafael Romero, Jarrito, Bernardo el de los Lobitos, and me. He told each of us what we should sing: El de la Matrona sang the authentic *serrana*; Almadén the *cantes de Chacón* ... each sang their specialty – I did the *malagueña del Mellizo, alegrías*, and *tientos*.

I remember that one of the French team was a blind recording engineer – you should have seen him. We would be practicing in the studio, and whenever someone hit a bad note, he'd tell us – didn't he ever have a good ear!

Later there were other anthologies – Mairena did his, Caracol, and so did Matrona, but ours was the first – the one that Perico and the French recorded.[25] It did incredibly well – particularly abroad – because it won an award from the French Academy and then it sold all over the world.

Once a Japanese rice merchant came to La Zambra and told us that seventy thousand anthologies had just gone on sale in Japan. Another time I ran into a reporter friend of mine – when he saw me, he gave me a big hug: "Pericón! I'm hugging you because you made me so happy!"

"What did I do?"

"Well, you see, I was in the Congo on an assignment. Who would have told me that even in the Congo, I'd hear an

---

[24] This first flamenco anthology [D-5] was recorded in the early 1950s, and released in 1954.

[25] Mairena's anthology is D-11, Caracol's is D-4, and Matrona's is D-12

alegrías de Cádiz? I'll never forget the joy it gave me when I heard it!"

The Dedication

After twenty years away from Cádiz, without ever returning, I finally went back. Right away my son Jumán started talking about a dedication.

First they gave me one in the *peña de Paco Herrera*, where they gave me their insignia. Then the Club Caleta presented me with a silver plaque. Finally came the official dedication in the Park Theater. They wanted to give me the proceeds, but when a reporter came and told me, I said I didn't want a cent of it, and they should give it all to retarded children.

There was a great lineup of artists – all getting paid except Caracol, who, when he found out about it, said to Aurelio de la Viesca: "Look – tell them to put me on the poster for Pericón's dedication – I'd love to sing there: first, because my father was from Cádiz, second, because Pericón is a dear friend, and third, because what he did for the retarded children can't be bought with money."

That night, after almost nine months without singing, he was in such good form that he sang for over an hour; the audience went crazy.

After the theater function was over, we had dinner in the *cortijo* Los Rosales, where Don Antonio Martín presented me with the Golden Rose to the applause of everyone. Around four in the morning, we all went to Vea Murguía, number 20, where I was born, where we found a commemorative plaque.[26] There was a great crowd – when I saw the plaque, I shouted:

---

[26] A year after Pericón's death, a street in the barrio de la Viña was named after him.

"Dear public, I'd like to ask a favor of the soul of Enrique el Mellizo – a moment of silence!"

The street was such that you couldn't hear a fly. Then Paquito de Lucía came playing the double *malagueña del Mellizo* and I sang with a strength that even surprised me. I finished amidst *oles* and applause – all at four in the morning.

Paquito and I hugged, he put away his guitar, and the people left – all to their homes – and I went with my grandchildren.

2. Stories from Cádiz — and ...

... *Its fiestas*

One year a ventriloquist came to Cádiz and did an automated puppet number. This gave someone from Cádiz the idea to put on an automated puppet show with real people – flamenco artists. He presented them at the Escudero Theater during Carnival.

The puppets all came out and sat down with their faces covered and strings tied to their bodies, from above, just like marionettes. The master came out, dressed in a ventriloquist uniform, and uncovered their painted faces, one by one. Following his instructions, the guitarists started playing, and then the singers, and finally the dancers. Always with marionette-like movements, but with such rhythm and art ...

The marionettes were Joselito el de la Rita, Antonio el Herrero, Habichuela, and others I don't remember – it's been so long ...

... *The old Carnivals*

The old Carnivals were really something! Those *chirigotas*, those choruses![27] On the day before Carnival all the *chirigotas*

---

[27] Cádiz is famous for its Carnival; several stories and descriptions figure into these tales. The style of the Carnival de Cádiz was influenced by the Venetian Carnival, and is similarly famous for masks, costumes. Central to the Carnival celebrations were the *chirigotas* or *murgas* - costumed singing groups who sing satirical songs; political and cultural satire is of paramount importance. These groups tour Cádiz on floats or, less formally, sing from bar to bar for free drinks and tips. The Carnival was suspended after the Civil War in 1937, and was revived in 1948 under the name *Fiestas Típicas de Cádiz*, but usually took place in May (to appease the Church).

and choruses competed for prizes at City Hall. Then they performed at the Falla Theater, charging admission because, of course, they'd never recoup all the money they spend on their costumes. But everything helped.

On the first day of Carnival, by six in the morning, the *murgas* were out, singing, dancing, drinking ... Later that night, they would get together in a bar and split the take. This went on for the first three days and on *Piñata Sunday*. All day there was singing and fun – with amazing wit and *gracia*. Groups made their way from Cruz Verde to Plaza de las Flores, stopping off at a bar called La Cabra to get ready and have a free drink before going to the plaza to sing among the stands – here, there – it was too much!

One of the most famous *chirigotas* was run by Suárez: seven or eight old geezers who drank everything they were given and more. Upon arriving at a bar they'd say:

Buenos días, don José,	Good Day don José,
le venimos a saludar;	we've come to greet you;
nos va a dar dos duros,	you'll give us two *duros,*
y encima la convidá.	and also a free drink.

They'd get their drink, go to another bar, then another, and another ... Of course, by two in the afternoon, two were missing, the next day they were down another three, and by the last day all that was left were the guy with the drum and the one with the castanets.

Suárez, who was a *murgista* until he was eighty, was the one who wrote the songs. One year he had a tall, blonde,

---

During the Franco dictatorship, the satire was heavily censored; hence, the songs relied on double meanings. In 1978, two years after Franco's death, Carnival was kicked off with a funeral procession, laying to rest the *Fiestas Típicas* and resuscitating the old *Carnaval de Cádiz*. Since these stories were collected in the early 1970s, Pericón is describing the pre-Franco Carnival. There is an extensive literature on the Carnival in Cádiz, for example Solís (1988) and Mintz (1997).

cross-eyed guy in the group, so he composed a verse that said:

En todo el mundo no s'encuentra	In all the world there is not found
un biscuzo tan divino,	such a divine squinter,
pues vino de los infiernos	come from the nether-worlds
en compañía de Tarquino,	along with Tarquino.
tiene la vista atravesá:	He only looks backwards:
valiente rato echaría su papá.	his father must have had a great time.

This same Suárez also composed this verse:

Es un campeón Suárez	Suárez is a champion
en ese del tiro al blanco,	in hitting the target;
es muy certero y seguro	he's a crack shot
con la chiquita del blanco,	at hitting the bull's eye.
tiene la vista de una acedía,	He's got a lazy eye,
la boca del pobre es una sala vacía.	And the poor guy's mouth is an empty room.

Because he had not a tooth in his head. Not one molar at all; but he was crazy about wine.

Other famous ones were the "Modernist Doctors", who one year sang this verse:

Para curar a España	To cure Spain
de sus dolencias,	of its ills
nosotros los doctores	we doctors
vamos a dar receta:	will give a prescription:
Se hace una caldera	put on a caldron
de doscientos metros	two hundred meters wide
y a todo que viva	and anyone who lives
de la política	off politics

se echa dentro.	gets thrown inside.
Cuando la caldera	When the caldron
bien repleta esté	is nice and full
se le arrima leña	bring on the firewood
y se deja ardiendo	and set it on fire
como un crepé.	like a crêpe.
Hay que tener cuidado	You have to be careful
y apercibirse	and watch out
que nadie de la olla	that no one
puede salirse,	escapes from the pot
que los hay tan pillos	because some of them are so crass
y tan granujas	and so slippery
que se van del caldero	that they'll get out of the caldron
aunque sea el agujero	even if the hole
el ojo de una aguja.	is like the eye of a needle.
Cuando ya esté hecho manteca	When they're melted down to lard
se le sacan los chicharones	get out the residue
y con esa pringue política	and with that political grease
se dan a España cuarenta unciones	Spain will get forty anointments
y a los treinta o cuarenta días	And in thirty or forty days
yo le puedo a usté asegurar	I can assure you
que la nueva patria española	that the new Spanish fatherland
ya se curó de su enfermedá	will be cured of its ills
y los españoles viven	and Spaniards will live
con toda tranquidá.	in peace.

They sang this in the middle of the street and no one said anything.

There was another chorus called "The Antiquarians" who sang an unbearably wonderful verse:[28]

Les presento aquí tres cuadros	I'm offering three paintings
del Zurbarán y del gran Murillo	by Zurbarán and the great Murillo.
que valen treinta mil duros	They're worth 30,000 *duros*
a precio de baratillo	at a bargain price,
y para venderlos pronto	but for a quick sale
yo los doy por la mitá.	I'll give you half off.
Representa el primero un edificio	The first one is of a building
donde un célebre turco	where a famous Turk
tuvo su harén en el siglo quinto,	kept his harem in the fifth century.
está entre Nicaragua y Panamá	It is between Nicaragua and Panama
un poquito a la izquierda del Paquistán.	A little to the left of Pakistan.
El segundo cuadro es un guacamayo	The second picture is of a parrot
que tuvo en su alcoba	that King Pelayo
el rey don Pelayo,	kept in his bedroom.
cuando más se mira	The more you look at it
más lejos se ve ,	the farther off it seems,
igual que el Castillo	just like the Castle
de Chuchurumbé.	of Chuchurumbé.[29]

---

[28] Pericón recorded this on D-8.

[29] El Castillo de *Chuchurumbé* is a Spanish children's poem with nested relative clauses, similar to *The House that Jack Built*, where the closer one gets to the Castle the more it recedes in fractal-like detail.

Y el último representa	The last one is a picture of
la copia de un gran sofá	the copy of a big couch
donde se sentaba Eva	where Eve sat
en compañía de Adán,	along with Adam.
y allí los dos muy tranquilos,	There they were relaxing,
no crean que esto es camaña,	and don't think I'm fooling;
en aquel gran paraíso	in that great paradise
cierto domingo por la mañana	one Sunday morning
los dos tenían mucha hambre	they were both real hungry,
y se comieron una manzana.	so they ate an apple.

This was composed by a poor bricklayer – they called him "Tío de la Tiza".[30]

    If anything of importance happened in Cádiz, come Carnival time they'd make up a song about it.

    The monument to the Cortés was under construction for at least six or seven years, with all the statues lying around and kids defecating on them ... so, one year they came out with this verse:[31]

Cuando dijieron que Cádiz	When they say
se ha de llamar	Cádiz should be called
la tacita de plata,	the little silver cup[32]
to el que dijo eso por la gloria Paco	Whoever says that, by Frank,

---

[30] He actually wasn't a poor bricklayer – rather he and his family owned several businesses in Cádiz.

[31] The Cortés monument, commemorating Spain's 1812 constitution, is in the Plaza de España. It was under construction between 1912 and 1929 (Peralta 2009:214).

[32] "*Tacita de plata*" or 'Little Silver Cup,' is a common sobriquet for Cádiz.

47

que metió la pata,	put his foot in it;
que se dé una vueltecita	he should take a stroll
por los barrios bajos sin adoquinados	through the unpaved slums.
y hasta con chichoneras salen por mandados.	you'll need a helmet to go out shopping,
Y si queréis distraerse	and if you want to be entertained
cuando haga Levante irse a Canalejas,	when there is an Easterly go to Canalejas;
que la que tenga añadío	whatever you've eaten,
por la gloria Paco allí se lo deja,	by Frank, you'll leave it there,
y eso que ahora no es nada	and that's nothing,
desde que le han puesto la reja.	now that they've put up the bars.
Si es la pescadería,	If you like to fish
vaya cosa preciosa:	you'll love this:
de todas las de España	in all Spain
es la más cochambrosa.	this is the filthiest.
En cambio el monumento	On the other hand, the monument
lo tienen tan cuidao	is so well maintained
que no hay una figura	that there isn't even one statue
que no parezca que s'ha purgao.	that doesn't look like it's been crapped on.

Because they were covered in crap up to the railings.

Then there were the costumes: I remember one year a wise guy came out announcing: "On *Piñata Sunday* at 3:00 in the afternoon, in the Plaza San Antonio, will appear the astronomer Tintín to discover the greatest phenomenon on Earth."

You should've seen – the plaza was packed with

people. Then, at five to three, they saw him coming down Buenos Aires Street. "Here comes the astronomer!"

And there came the astronomer Tintín with his robe covered with comets and stars, his astronomer's hat, and a big, scary apparatus. He walked to the middle of the plaza – everyone was waiting for the greatest phenomenon on Earth.

"Ladies and Gentlemen! I salute Cádiz before discovering the greatest phenomenon on Earth!"

He started to look through the apparatus – he looked and looked and looked ... People were saying: "What could it be?" "What is it?"

Finally the guy got up and said "Here it is! The greatest phenomenon on Earth!"

And he had crapped in the middle of the plaza; he was naked under his robe and while looking through the telescope he took a dump – that was the greatest phenomenon on Earth.

The beggars also had their tricks: one would go out pretending to be a bootblack, passing through the terraces. If he caught you sitting and you offered your shoe, he took out a can of tar and a brush – of course, when you saw that it was a practical joke, you gave him a *peseta* to go away and look for other shoes.

All of Cádiz was packed with people – the streets – the coaches. The coaches started off on La Rosa Street, then El Corrlón, Callejones Cardoso, Cruz Verde, Robles Street, Plaza de las Flores, and Compañía Street, until Plaza San Juan de Dios. One coach after another – one horse's head on the bumper of the next coach. They threw streamers and confetti from all the coaches – entire packages of streamers and confetti by the bagful – almonds, anise, pine nuts ...

We were up on the coaches throwing confetti and streamers just like the rich men. La Habana was the bar we hung out in – one coach after another would stop:

"Pericón! Find a guitarist and come up with us!"

So – off to sing in the coaches. I'd finish with one party and back to La Habana. In a few minutes another coach stopped: "Pericón!"

So it was Pericón in the coach again. It was this way for the three days of Carnival: the only sleep was a few short naps on a table and then on to the coaches, the singing, the wine... Of course, we also got to have fun with the streamers and confetti just like the rest.

Then finally came *Piñata Sunday* with the dance in the Principle Theater, with all the boxes full of parties and all the parties wanting *cante*. I arrived at three of four in the morning and right away:

"Pericón! Come up here!"

Up in the boxes I'd sing *bulerías, alegrías, tanguillos*, and stuff like that.

Boy did they ever mix it up! When everyone was there, they started throwing the girls off the balconies – the girls they picked up to bring to the parties.

"Hey so and so!" They'd shout to those below, "here she comes!"

You should have seen the poor girls flying through the theater.

At five in the morning they had the *piñata* – a girl dressed as an angel, which they brought out in the middle of the theater, down from the celling, throwing handfuls of candy and bonbons.

... The festivals

Every year each neighborhood of Cádiz celebrated their festival: in La Viña: Santa María, El Mentidero, and La Libertad. You should've seen how they decked out the neighborhood – because they gave prizes to the best decorated patios and balconies. Some patios had dances and everyone had a great time. In La Viña they put up a *tablao* on Corralón Street; every night of the festival they had *cante* – two or three singers, with tables set up so people could drink and listen. In El Mentidero it was pretty much the same – you'd go down Hércules Street, Las Navas, Plaza de Falla, ... There was a really tall tree in the Plaza de Falla, and to make it even taller, they put a long stick on top of it, with a light bulb on the end. It looked like a star. All the streets were lined with lanterns, garlands, and streamers. In the Plaza de Mentidero they also had a *tablao* for *cante flamenco*.

Later came the festival in La Libertad. They also had their *tablao* in the Plaza Las Flores – endless lanterns along Sagasta Street, Los Callejones, and San Juan Street.

Finally came the festival in Santa María; it was the best – those decorated houses, those patios – and in almost every patio there was *cante flamenco,* dancing, everything ...

I remember the shrimp cakes they sold on Soperanis Street. The cakes were as big as a Basque beret and cost a *perra chica.* Of course, if you arrived with a peseta, you had enough to invite a whole regiment.

... The Christ of Santa María

During Cádiz' Holy Week, the bearers who carried the floats were famous.[33] These were men from the docks who were able to carry Christ with such a rhythm, that one was moved at the way He had such a life-like gait. One year the Christ of *Santa*

---

[33] Holy Week in Spain is a major festival which features a procession of penitents following floats of the Virgin and Christ. These floats, which are very heavy and ornate, are carried by a group of *cargadores* ('bearers') – strong men who specialize in giving the floats movement that makes them more life-like.

María came out, carrying his cross and wearing his tunic.[34] The rope around the tunic had two light bulbs on the end, which swayed back and forth to the rhythm of the bearers. The Christ came out of the church and went down Soperanis Street. Everyone expected the light bulbs to break, because the street was so narrow, and with the swaying and the balconies, they couldn't have made it through intact. But no – they didn't break. They came out to the Plaza San Juan de Dios without breaking the bulbs: they went in and out between iron bars and balconies without breaking, because of the beautiful and measured gait of the bearers.

You should have seen when the Christ came out of the church! The streets and bars were packed with people drinking wine. At two in the morning, everyone went to Campo del Sur to wait for the Christ to come up the Calesas hill. He came up to the entrance to the jail, facing the door, while the penitents moved away. Christ was left alone, with that Gypsy face and the wind blowing His long hair; four civil guards were on the side, and all of the prisoners inside were singing *saetas* ...

Then back to the church in Santa María; upon arriving, that was the climax. It would be three or four in the morning and packed with people everywhere – fifty or seventy people singing *saetas* without stopping – first one, then another, and another ... When it was time to take Him inside, and they started to move Him, no one let them, so He stayed another three or four hours.

Because, of course, no one minded staying until whatever time, asking for miracles, singing *saetas*, rocking Him, rocking Him ...

Because they had such a strong faith in Him and in His

---

[34] Each float is associated with a particular church – this Christ, El Nazareno, is from the Iglesia de Santa María, in the barrio de Santa María. Noted for long, flowing, authentic human hair and a dark complexion, it is favored by the *Gitanos* of Santa María.

miracles; they even believed that His nails and hair grew.

... Its quirks

In barrio Santa María there was the funniest thing: there they sold meat called "underwear meat". It came from the underwear of the guys who worked in the slaughterhouse. When they were ready to send out an order, they'd cut off pieces of beef, and stuff it in their underwear, where it would fall down – the old fashioned underwear that came to their angles. They took it home to their wives to sell in the street: "Underwear meat!"

You should have seen the meat – the best veal that would have cost three or four *duros* per kilo in the market – but they sold it for twelve *pesetas* – and it was the same meat!

... The pregones

When I was a kid in Cádiz, they sold a lot of things on the street with *pregones*. I mean, no matter what they were selling, they'd go along singing about it in such a way that, even if you didn't want to, you'd buy one just to hear the *pregón*.

There was a guy from a village that came selling all kinds of herbs; he had a beautiful *pregón*, which he sang with such a voice and melody:

Llevo	I have
la hierba luisa,	the herb louisa,
pa los dolores d'estómago. Llevo	for stomach aches. I have
la flor de la Pili,	Pili's flower
pa los canariros que no cantan,	for canaries that won't sing
pa que sean ruiseñores.	so they can be nightingales.

Y también llevo la hierba militi,	I also have the militi herb
pa los meses deteníos.	for menstrual periods.

You should have seen the commotion: all the women on their periods:
> "Ay, come here!"
> "Give me a handful!"
> "Give me a handful of the *militi!*"
> In that way he sold the entire tray of herbs.

Then there was the guy who sold water. Even if you weren't thirsty, you'd drink five or six glasses without realizing it. He stood in the Plaza San Antonio, in front of a silent movie theater. All of us kids, going to the theater, would buy his water. "Waterie", he'd say, and start singing:

Ayyyyyyy,	Ayyyyyy,
agüitiii	waterie,
frequitiii	coldie,
bibibibibibi	drinkie, Drinkie, drinkie.
¿Quién quiere un vasito?	Who wants a glass?

One would come by, and another, and another, to drink water. When the guy saw that you almost finished a glass, he'd start again:

Ayyyyyyy,	Ayyyyyy,
agüitiii,	waterie,
agüitiii,	waterie,
agüitiii,	waterie.
fresquita como la nieve.	Cold as snow.

And something would happen that made you drink five or six glasses without meaning to. So, "Waterie" sold three or four

jugs of water every night at a *perra chica* a glass.
They also sold flowers on the street with *pregones* –
anything they had, they'd sell with *pregones*.
There was another guy with hard-boiled eggs. He filled
a big basket full of eggs; later he painted them red, green,
yellow, ... He stood in the doorway of the School of the
Brothers, selling his painted eggs at a *perra chica* an egg. I
remember that this guy played a game with his painted eggs
called "you hit me or I hit you" – it went like this:
You'd come take an egg and he'd say: "You hit me or I
hit you?"
And you'd say: "I hit you." or "You hit me."
Depending on what you said, you hit your egg against
one of the eggs he chose, or he hit his against yours. If his
shell cracked first, then your egg was free. But the guy wasn't
stupid – the kids' eggs always cracked first because his wasn't
really an egg – it was a wooden egg painted to look like the
others, and, of course, it never cracked. One egg, another, and
with the game, he had all the kids hooked.

... Gallegos and Montañeses

In Cádiz, between the *Gallegos* and the *Montañeses*, they
owned practically everything. The stores – well it was a rare
one that wasn't either owned or run by a *Montañés*, and
Gallegos ran the fried fish shops. The water carriers and the
garbage men were also *Gallegos* ... In fact, I really gave it to
those guys when I was a kid. They'd go along Campo del Sur
with their donkey carts when I'd suddenly appear with my two
hundred kids.
"Let's go after the carts!"
You should have seen it – all the kids throwing rocks
and the *Gallegos* running off with their carts. Kids' stuff!

I don't know what it was about the *Montañeses* and the *Gallegos*, but whenever one of them opened a store/bar, it was a sure success. If someone from Cádiz opened up, he'd have to sell it to a *Gallego* or a *Montañeses* within two months.[35] I remember a funny thing about this:

Two bars were sold in the Plaza de las Flores: one to a *Gallego* and another to someone from Cádiz. The *Gallego* opened his business and started giving out great *tapas*. People would then go to the Cádiz-run bar and would only get a little piece of cheese or a few olives – of course they started to say: "Man, it's not worth coming here with these *tapas*, compared to what they give next door."

The poor guy from Cádiz was going crazy over the *tapas*. Until one morning he got pissed; he opened the bar, and whenever someone ordered a *valdepeñas*, which cost three *perras gordas*, he gave them back a *peseta* as a *tapa* – he gave it to them on a plate. When people saw that and asked "what's this?", he replied: "That? That's your *tapa* – so you can't say the *Gallego* gives better *tapas* than me!"

... Bars and brothels

I remember when I was young and starting to break into the flamenco scene, there were two groups: the one on Rosa Street and the one on Aguaúcho. On Rosa Street were two bars: La Habana and The 606 – those were where we younger guys hung out: El Churringui, El Peste, El Niño de la Isla – who they called "Isla" – and some other singers. The guitarists were Antonio el Herrero, Paco el Jilguerito, and Habichuelita – the nephew of Juan Gandulla. In Aguaúcho you'd find the

---

[35] Pericón uses the word *tienda* 'store', which I translate as 'bar'. In his time, and still today in some cases, establishments doubled as small grocery stores and bars. One still hears the expression *Montañés* to refer to a grocery store, as in *"Lo compré en el Montañés"* – 'I bought it at the store.'

older artists: the singers were El Toni, Chiclanita, Antonio el Mellizo, El Morcilla, and Aurelio. The guitarists were El Pollo and Capinetti.

These places are where we went at night to wait for the coaches with *señoritos* from Cádiz or sailors in order to get a party together and make some money. Such was the way of life: some paid only a little and others were very good to us. That's why when *señoritos* came looking for a party, if we knew a ship had come to port, we'd say: "Look, we can't because we're already contracted by some sailors."

It was a lie, but it was better to wait for the sailors than to have a party with a tightwad. Of course, we were waiting for this engineer, that steward, the other officer ... great *aficionados* who were lavish – they brought lots of money and they spent it.

In those days it was the boats that gave Cádiz its ambience: the Balbanera, the Montserrat, the Buena Esperanza, with routes to New York or Habana, which brought lots of tourists to Cádiz. They came for the sights, the Phoenician stuff, and everything. [36] When the tourists arrived, there were a bunch of guys called *pupileros* who took the tourists to the brothels to party.

These *pupileros* would first find out how the voyage had been; then they'd mix with the passengers, pretending to be one of them: "What a passage through the Gulf of León! For a minute there, I thought I'd had it, and wouldn't ever see my Cádiz again!"

"Oh – you're from Cádiz?" the real passenger said.

"Oh yeah – I know it like the palm of my hand. In fact, I seem to remember that there is a brothel around here – we

[36] Cádiz is the oldest city in Western Europe, founded by the Phoenicians around 1100 BC. However, given its strategic location, it has been destroyed many times, and relatively little remains in the way of ancient ruins.

could go and have some fun."

That way, he hooked them and took them to a brothel. When they got there, the madam took them to a room and brought out the girls, the wine, and called us. We went – a singer and a guitarist – there was *cante*, girls, and wine, until finally the *pupilero* said: "Well, Gentlemen, I've had enough for today; let's get the check."

He called the madam; she came in; he asked for the check and she said: "Well, with the girls, the guitarist, the singer, the wine and everything, it comes to to 70, 90, or 100 pesos"... whatever it was. The *pupilero* did the accounts and said: "It comes to this much apiece."

Everyone paid their share, including the *pupilero* and they all left. Of course, the *pupilero* was back in a half hour for his commission.

There were lots of places like that – until Maestre came in – a very stern governor who put an end to it all. He closed down the brothels and everything and confused everything. Because he tried to stop something that has been around forever in God's world and ruined us artists.

... The girls

Before Maestre came in, whenever someone would come to La Habana looking for artists for a party, they'd then ask where they could find some girls. Since we knew the score, we'd tell them: "Look, in this house, there's so-and-so, and in that other house ..."

We went to pick them up; the *señorito* took her out and brought her to the *venta* for the party.

The most famous madam was La Barquillera, who had at least seven or eight brothels: one on Herrador Street, four or five on Soledad Street, and another on La Plata Street ... so – a bunch of brothels. In each one she had seven, ten, twelve girls between eighteen and twenty. You should have seen the girls ... But not only La Barquillera; there were other famous ones too: Rosita, the Captain, and others I've forgotten.

Most of the girls didn't do anything – that is, they didn't dance or sing. But a few sang a little and danced in their own way. There was one called the Captain, who was a demon from Hell – with a voice beyond compare, and knowing how to hold her own and keep up with everyone drinking – by the time she got tipsy, you were falling down drunk. What a woman – and beautiful!

There were others like her, with style and faces that drove you crazy: La Montenegro, La Carola, La Fidela, ... who on top of being real women, were really friendly and knew how to hang out and drink. Of course, these were the ones in most demand.

One of them was called La Tani – she wasn't from Cádiz – she was from Granada. We gave her that name because of a song she sang: "*Ay, Tani, que mi Tani, que mi Tani...*"[37]

You should have seen her when she put her hair down – it came to her butt – and she started singing and dancing to that song. You'd die. The *señoritos* took her out to party every night. We loved her too, because whenever they hired her, she said they needed to hire a guitarist and a singer, too.

But life is like this: About twenty years after her prime – one night we were partying – Luis el Compare, Antonio el Herrero, and me – we were with Enriquito the photographer. He got it in his head to go to La Línea, so we went. At one in the morning we showed up at a brothel run by La Puerca. We knocked on the door, and when I saw who opened, I died! Her eyebrows and eyelashes had fallen out; she was bald; her face disfigured ... I thought to myself: "My God! If you could see

---

[37] This chorus is sung on D-8 ("*Robaron un cobertor*").

her twenty years ago compared to how she is today!"

...*The coaches*

In Cádiz back then there was the custom of having parties in the horse-drawn coaches. Instead of going into a room to listen to singing, most people rented a coach and drove around Cádiz so that everyone could see that they – so-and-so of whoever – were having a party with three or four artists.

So we artists spent all night singing here and there. We would drive up to this bar or the other – since everything was always open and there was always wine – the coach stopped at the door, and we didn't even have to get down from the coach – the *Montañés* brought us the wine. We continued on from bar to bar, or to a girl's house for a serenade, playing and singing all the way. I remember a bunch of times when it got to be three or four in the morning and we stopped somewhere to keep on singing – before we knew it, all the balconies were full of women with their husbands, the men in their nightshirts and the women in white nightgowns, listening to us. When we were about to move on, they'd shout:

"No! Don't take them away!"

"Stay a little longer!"

"Sing another, Pericón!"

So, of course, the *señorito* let us stay a little longer.

Back then there were various companies that rented coaches: Don Teodoro Simón in the Plaza San Juan de Dios, Constantino Paredes in the Plaza Candelaria; in the Paseo Canalejas there were two – Barquillero and Cubiella – and in Plaza San Antonio there were two more – Niño de la Isla and Diego Mateo. Overall a good number of coaches. Some, like the ones from Diego Mateo and Niño de la Isla, came with liveried coachmen and everything. The types of coaches were the Blackbird, Coupé, Berlin, and the Landau. Everyone asked for the type of coach best suited to them, but also their favorite coachman. There were some famous coachmen who everyone wanted: one named El Pájaro who was famous; Rafael el Cuentista was also really famous – always very serious in his Landau with two horses. Then there were others who even danced, while driving the horses, like Linaza, who sang *fandangos* right there on his perch with such *gracia*.

Then there was Manolete, who knew all the verses from the old choruses and *comparsas*. Finally, El Tripa, who also danced really well and Verbena, who liked a glass of wine better than all the parties in the world ...

... *It's juergas*

On the corner near La Habana, there was a *sereno* who relied on his tricks to bring more home.

When we came home from our *juergas* with a *señorito*, he'd signal to us to get the *señorito* to buy him a drink. When he got his drink, instead of spirits or brandy, he'd drink a cup of water with coffee that was supposed to be brandy, or plain water that stood in for spirits.

Then, in the morning, before going back to City Hall, he stopped by La Habana, and for each drink, they gave him a roll – with the thirty four or thirty five rolls he got everyday, he went home happy, taking them to his kids.

... *Those fiestas*

There was this guy in Cádiz who, whenever he had a *fiesta*, he didn't care if it went for three or four days. He came to the Aguaúcho and the first thing he'd do was send for three or four women. As soon as they arrived he'd tell them: "None of this 24 hour stuff – whoever goes in with me comes out with me." Then he'd call the artists he knew didn't mind being there for as long as it took. When everyone was assembled it was up to the room, with two or three crates of wine, a ham, a bucket, and a mattress. He closed the door and gave the owner instructions not to disturb him and not open the door until he rang the bell.

Then the party started: singing, dancing, this, the other, and he didn't let anyone leave. If someone got drunk and had to throw up – the bucket. If someone got tired and needed to sleep – the mattress. But he never laid down for anything in the world. He sat with his head on the table – a half hour later he said: "Ok – let's have a drink."

This was the strongest guy I've ever seen at partying. He never got tired: singing, women, wine ...

Later, when I moved to Madrid, I had the fortune to have a long party like that – it had been going three days by the time I got there. I was at the bar when I saw Niño Valdepeñas come out. He called me: "Hey you! Have you ever sung for Don Francisco Gálvez?"

"No"

"Well come on – you'll sing for him tonight."

Of course I was thrilled, starving as I was. We went in the room and Niño Valdepeñas said to him: "Don Francisco, I want to introduce to you a kid who just came from Cádiz – you're going to like the way he sings."

"Ok – let's see."

I came out singing and they ate me up. I sang two or three verses of *alegrías*, and Don Francisco got up, gave me a hug, and two thousand *pesetas*. Hungry as I was, was I ever glad to see the money! Don Francisco said:

"You can leave if you want"

And El Niño Valdepeñas: "No! Don't leave!"

And me: "Right! I'm leaving!"

The party went on, singing, more singing, wine ... Two hours later, this guy pulled out another two thousand, dividing it among the artists, along with cigars, tobacco, and everything. Since I was used to the coaches in Cádiz, I thought I'd gone crazy.

But I wasn't crazy – I had just come across a guy who liked to support artists and didn't mind spending thirty or forty thousand *duros* in a party. He came often to the Villa Rosa, and hired everyone there. Then he passed out handfuls of money to the twelve or fourteen he'd hired – what a case!

... *Espadrille artists*

A sailor named Don José Marón used to go often to La Habana – he was delirious about *cante*. But he had this quirk, and unless you went along with it, you didn't sing.

When he arrived at La Habana, he would go into the room and when Pedro, the owner, came up, he'd say: "Get me some espadrille artists."

Pedro came down and told us: "José Marón is upstairs and wants espadrille artists – as you know, if you want to sing, go buy some espadrilles."

Since José Marón paid well and also treated us very well, we went to a store and bought some espadrilles made of hemp, that cost six *perras gordas*. When we got back, we left our shoes downstairs, went upstairs, knocked on the door where Don José was, and before he let us in, we'd have to show him our feet with the espadrilles on.

That's how it was, time after time. What we did was leave pairs of espadrilles in La Habana, and whenever Don José showed up, we'd get them out, because if you didn't wear espadrilles, there was no party.

... The park thieves

I spent a lot of time at La Habana with a crippled singer named Jacinto; you should have seen how funny he was – looking for thieves. This was because there was this short little *señorito* who made a lot of money and spent it on us looking for thieves. He came by La Habana, and if we weren't in a party, he'd come right up to Jacinto and me to go to the park and hunt for thieves. He gave us each a knife, and once at the park, I'd say: "Look! I think one is moving behind that tree."

"Let me! Let me first! I'll get him!"

Of course, since it was a lie, the *señorito* ran to the tree and found nothing.Then either me or Jacinto would jump in: "Well, I saw a shadow, but you must have scared him and he escaped through the fence."

We did two or three rounds of the park and when the *señorito* got tired of it, we went back La Habana, where he gave us each two *duros*, and said: "Man, we didn't have much luck today – let's see if we have better luck tomorrow and we catch one."

It went on like that with this *señorito* for over a month looking for thieves in the park – playing along with his quirk of wanting to hunt for thieves. Finally we got sick of his obsession, and we planted one of Jacinto's cousins behind a tree – a longshoreman – in order to cure the *señorito* forever of his need to hunt for thieves. We told Jacinto's cousin to wait in a certain place at night, and when the *señorito* showed up the wise-guy Jacinto said: "I think we'll find one tonight."

"Let's see. Let's see if we have some luck tonight."

The three of us went to the park with our knives ready; we came to a place near where Jacinto's cousin was, and I said: "Careful! There is a shadow moving there!"

And the *señorito*: "Stay back! Let me! I'll go first – I'm the one who needs to catch him."

And he went crouching down with his knife, with us behind, waiting. When he got to the tree, the cousin jumped out, stood in front of him and knocked the poor *señorito* silly. We took off running, pretending to be after the thief. When we got back to La Habana, the *señorito* said: "What! You didn't catch him? I almost had him!"

"Well, you see ... it's that he ran real fast."

We had to share the ten *duros* the *señorito* gave us with the cousin ...

... A basket of sea urchins

We had a friend who was the biggest *aficionado* in the world. His name was Enrique, and since he was a photographer, we called him Enrique the photographer. Every Saturday, when this Enrique finished work, he came looking for us for a party. He called Antonio el Herrero as the guitarist, and for singers, Luis el Compare and me. We loved it, because it meant we had sure work on Saturdays. Also, he treated us really well – gave us whatever we wanted and was very gracious.

But I tell you! Once he got started, it was impossible to stop him – hour after hour, until five or six on Sunday afternoon! Since he didn't have to work, he didn't mind being there until whenever, but it was killing us – singing, drinking, ... Until one day I had an idea. It was around eight in the morning, we were dead tired, unable to go on, so I said: "Enrique, I bet you couldn't eat a whole basket of sea urchins."

"What do you mean I can't?"

So we went and got the urchins – you should have seen, at least forty dozen urchins, and with the way urchins make you sleepy ... We finished them off, and the poor guy lost all of his desire to keep partying; he paid us, kissed us goodbye – he loved us a lot – and until next Saturday.

It was that way every time we saw that he was going to go on until the next day: "Enrique, let's have some sea urchins."

... El Vivillo

When the ships form the Cádiz Company came to port, I went to a bar called El Zoco, that was in the Cathedral Plaza, next to another place called La Mezquita.[38] There in El Zoco I often ran into the guitarist Perico Pavón, who'd say: "Pericón, don't leave – a boat came in and they'll probably call us."

That was when the *pupileros* picked up the passengers and took them to the brothels.

I remember during one of those parties, there was a man alone with the *pupilero*. He was short, stout, there with his guide, two bottles of wine, and two girls, drinking. We went in, sat down, and sang ... after about three hours of partying, this guy asked for the bill. When the madame brought it, he got up and said: "Madame, doesn't this seem a little steep?"

"No, *señor*, we don't rob anyone here."

"You're right about that – I'm the only robber here – I'm El Vivillo."

And it really was El Vivillo, who had arrived from Buenos Aires and it just happened that I sang for him. You should have seen the madame, when she realized who he was – she fixed the bill – reducing it by half. He paid, left, and I was there thinking: "El Vivillo! I just sang for El Vivillo in the flesh!" Because at that time that guy was so famous.

... As tourists

There was a sailor in *San Fernando* that was crazy about me.

---

[38] See Part 1, note 19.

This guy's name was don Sebastián Nogá, and on a thousand occasions, without having to sing or anything, he gave me money for the house.

Once, when we were in a *fiesta*, it turned out that el Lepanto had docked. Since I was always bugging him about wanting to see the inside of one of those ships, and we were three sheets, he said "Pericón – I'll show you the ship."

So off we went looking for el Lepanto: don Sebastián, a girl he'd picked up at the Petí Kursal, and me. We got on board, saw the ship, and then off to his stateroom to continue the party – a whiskey, another whiskey, me singing ... before we knew it, it was eight in the morning.

A sailor came running up saying: "Captain! The commander just arrived!"

You should have seen the captain – even though he loved to party, when it came to work, he was very serious. With the commander there, he didn't know what to do with us – until I had an idea: "Look don Sebastián, me and the girl can pretend to be tourists and you can pretend to show us the boat."

So we did – he gave me a camera, and we came out of the stateroom with him showing us the boat: "The smokestack" – "Oh – the smokestack!"

"The prow" – "Oh – the prow!"

"The stern" – "Oh – the stern!"

Until we got to the portal – he shook our hands politely, and we said: "Oh – *muchasss graciasss, muchasss graciasss!*"

And we left down the gangway to the Plaza San Juan de Dios.

... The store

When I worked in Café X in San Fernando, I made some very good friends. When they had a party on the Island, they'd come to Cádiz to bring me back with them. I'd spend some time with them, and then, around five or six in the morning, everyone went home – except me, who was left waiting for the tram. Until one day I said I'd love to come to San Fernando – but they had to take me back. Of course, most of them said no – they didn't like the idea of two trips – one to take me back and another back home – after a *juerga*.

But there was one *Montañés* who thought better. He'd come to Cádiz around midnight, find me in La Habana, and we'd start the party either there or in the Tres Reyes or in Corona. Then, a little after five in the morning, he'd say: "Pericón – come back to San Fernando with me – I want to invite you to my house."

And there went Pericón with the *Montañés* to his house – which wasn't even a house – it was his store. He opened the store, I started singing, and pretty soon the place filled up with women doing their shopping – with me singing like a gramophone – until ten in the morning, when I'd say: "So what's going on – when am I going back to Cádiz?"

"Right now – whenever you want."

Then he'd give me a kilo of rice, of garbanzos, and of beans, on top of paying me. Since the situation was always so bad, I put up with singing behind the counter in order to go home with food. That's life.

... Two thousand five hundred and two

I had a doctor friend in Cádiz – an *aficionado* like the rest, who had the same defect as Enriquito the photographer. Once in a *fiesta*, he'd forget the hours, the days ... Since I lived off of this, I had to put up with it, so as not to lose the clientele.

I remember once we were at a *venta* drinking wine. It was about two in the afternoon and we had been partying since the night before.

A car pulled up – a kid got out and looked around; then

said to the doctor: "Hey – I need you to come with me."
"Why? What's the matter?"
"It's my mother – she has a terrible pain."
"OK – right away."
So off they went – the kid and the doctor – after forty hours of *juerga* – to see the sick woman. The doctor got to the house and the whole family was there waiting. They all went to the woman's room; the doctor said to the son "wait out here and leave me alone with her." Then he said to the woman "start counting until I tell you to stop."

The old woman started counting – five minutes passed, then fifteen, then, when it had been nearly an hour, the worried son opened the door: There was the poor lady with the doctor asleep on her chest, still counting: "Two thousand five hundred and two, two thousand five hundred and three, two thousand five hundred and four, two thousand five hundred and five, ..."

... *The peseta trick*

Back then, in the summer, Antonio el Herrero and me would go to a fair in a little town outside Cádiz. We were contracted by a guy name el Colorao, who had a little *venta* on the outskirts.

I remember one year I got the idea of doing some slight of hand tricks. It was such a hit that the next year they announced that Antonio el Herrero was going to play the morning bells on the guitar at dawn on August fifteenth, and that night, in the *venta*, after singing, I would do slight of hand.[39]

And so it was – at five in the morning on that day there were five or six hicks assembled saying "Let's hear those morning bells!" Antonio was asleep. "Come on Antonio! Get

---

[39] August 15th is the day of the Virgin Mary.

the guitar and play something, or they'll kill us with tomatoes tonight!"

So Antonio picks up the guitar and plays something resembling morning bells, and they all left happy. That night we worked on a stage they had put up. We finished, got down, and they started: "What about the slight of hand tricks?"

"Slight of hand!"

"We want tricks!"

Even though I didn't want to – the tricks were really only something I did for friends – but I didn't have any choice but to get back up on stage to do some tricks.

"Dear Public! Dear Public! The owner of this establishment will give five hundred *pesetas* – five HUNDRED *pesetas*! - to anyone who is able to do what I do."

"Do you see this *peseta*? You see it? Well I can put it on my forehead – stuck to my forehead – see how it stays put? And now see how – without touching it – it falls on its own!"

Of course, by stretching my forehead, the *peseta* that was stuck there fell off.

"See how easy it is? Well the owner will give five hundred pesetas to anyone who dares to try and who can do the same as me!"

You should have seen it – this hick got up with a forehead that looked like it could knock down a house. I got the *peseta*, and with much theater, pushed it on real hard (the trick is that by pushing hard, it feels like it is there, but the *peseta* stays stuck to my finger).

"Let's see – let's see if this gentleman is able to drop the *peseta* without touching it!"

You should have see the hick, with his huge forehead, making all kinds of faces – the people laughed and laughed – and the hick made more faces. Finally he thought "they're pulling my leg!" and he felt with his hand that there was no *peseta*. He was pissed and came after me like he wanted to kill

70

me! The hick!

... When Maestre came

When Maestre came in as governor and ordered everything to close at midnight, we were broken. A capital like Cádiz, used to having doors open at all hours, to have *juergas* and drink wine whenever ... We were ruined – we kept saying "now we'll all starve."

In order to survive we had to do what we could. If a *señorito* came wanting a party, calling me and whoever else, first we snuck into a store for wine, and then went to the beach ... We sat down on the sand: the *señoritos*, the girls, the guitarist, and the singer, and had the party right there on the beach – wine, singing, *juerga* ...

Sometimes a policeman would come by to tell us we couldn't be there – we invited him to have a drink, befriended him, and that way we could continue to earn a living.

When it wasn't the beach, we got in a horse-drawn coach, went out to the country along Campo del Sur, to Puerta Tierra, with the wine inside the coach, stopping here and there in the middle of nowhere.

... Its Characters

In Cádiz there was a mason named Galindo; you should have heard how he sang *siguiriyas* – with an *eco*, a strength, with knowledge. Even singing as he did, he never sang for anyone or went to *fiestas* – nothing. He would get together with five or six mason friends, drink six bottles of red wine, and in one bar, another bar, they passed the night listening to his *cante*.

... *Ignacio Ezpeleta*[40]

We had a club in Cadiz solely dedicated to listening to Ignacio; every afternoon, when it was time for coffee,[41] about four of us got together in the Turisbar: Aurelio, Paco Añote, Capinetti, Charol, me, plus another three or four, to wait for Ignacio, to hear what he had to say.

Ignacio Ezpeleta was a Gypsy with a gift of gab

We were ready for him when he arrived. When he sat down someone would start a conversation designed to bring out Ignacio's humor – a natural *gracia* that was not learned, but something he carried inside. We all stayed quiet listening to him because, of course, that's what we wanted – to listen to the things he said – we passed four hours drooling over the things – just listening to the things Ignacio would say.

His favorite topics were medicine and illnesses; when you'd least expect it, he'd say very seriously: "Yeah – that's true, but I'll tell you something you don't know: the tuberculosis microbe is conspiring with the National Police..."

That was his *gracia* – no one expected the whoppers he'd come up with. Furthermore, he never laughed or anything – he'd come out with a whopper bigger than the cathedral, and remain calm and serious, as if he'd said 2+2 = 4. He talked about medicine, politics, or whatever – that was the gift he had.

I remember another afternoon when we were also on the topic of illnesses and he jumped in: "Don't say anything else about that! Nothing else! It makes me think of my son

---

[40] Ignacio Espeleta – the text spells his name with a 'z' to indicate the Andalucian *ceceo* [lisp].

[41] Around 5:00 PM, after the *siesta*, Spain's cities come to life as people go out to shop, drink coffee, etc.

José!"

"What happened to your son José?"

"*Hombre*, my son José was born mute; my wife and I were devastated: 'Ay, what has God sent us! What a horrible thing! He sent us with this mute child!' Both of us horrified – 'Forget it! He came out mute!' And mute he was until age fourteen, when he broke his silence. He saw a pile of prickly pears – one of them was so big that it made an impression, so he said: 'Papá, I want that prickly pear.' So of course, I bought him the prickly pear."

And then he sang with a compás and a gracia that took your breath away

There's one thing recorded in my memory that I'll never forget – and it is from more than fifty years ago.

I was in the door of La Habana when I saw horse drawn coach with Ignacio and El Morcilla singing *alegrías*. They were keeping time, each with two huge spoons. My God! When those two got out of the coach doing *compás* with the spoons and singing *alegrías*, I died! What a way to do it! I'll never forget.

He had his own way of singing; a personal take on the *cantes*. That *salida* of the *alegrías*;[42] those *bulerías*; that facility of fitting anything into the rhythm. Even the *guajiras* he fit perfectly into *bulerías*:

Como quieres que yo a ti te abra	How do you mean for me to open
la puerta de me bujío,	the door to my hut?
si la mulata está dentro,	My mulata is inside
dueña del corazon mío...	She owns my heart...[43]

[42] Ignacio Espeleta is credited with developing the now traditional "*ti-tiri tran-tran*" *alegrías salida*; see Appendices.

[43] Pericón recorded this on D-7.

In spite of being such an artist, he didn't live from it. He worked in the slaughterhouse, like Antonio el Mellizo and El Morcilla.   If a good *aficionado*, like Sánchez Mejías, wanted to hear him, they had to find him in the slaughterhouse.

Sánchez Mejías went to the slaughterhouse, watched Ignacio kill cows, later they went to a *fiesta*. He'd have him singing for two days, give him a ham, and Ignacio would go home happy. It was because of his friendship with Sánchez Mejías that Ignacio was contracted for the *Las Calles de Cádiz*.

And he'd never worked in a theater

The first one who put on *Las Calles de Cádiz* was La Argentinita and Sánchez Mejías. Since they knew the Cádiz scene so well, they talked to Ignacio about playing the role of the shoemaker. At first he didn't want to, but Sánchez Mejías convinced him: "Don't be silly, Ignacio; all you'll need to do is sing *alegrías* twice and the *tanguillo* about the Plaza del Catedral. You come out with your leather apron, your hammer, and your shoe-mold ..."

When they played in Paris, the curtain went up; he walked out alone with his hammer and mold, and he got this incredible ovation. And he'd never worked in a theater before!

Of course, he also was up to his tricks.

Rafael Ortega told me that one night it was five minutes before curtain and Ignacio was nowhere to be found. It was a hot summer night, and, of course, since Rafael knew him, he went to the bathroom. There he found Ignacio in the bathtub: "*Hombre*, Ignacio, it's time to go on."

"Time? Are you saying we're going to go on in this heat?"

Ezpeleta was a Gypsy who couldn't fit through a door: strong, huge, and did he eat!

I remember a *fiesta* in San Severiano with this don José from the Transatlantic Company. I don't know why, but he put on a dinner and invited some of us artists, Espeleta, too. You should have seen him eat: he ate entire cans of anchovies with a spoon – he put the spoon in one end, and pushed the anchovies out the other, emptying the can.

That day there happened to be a mysterious *señorito* at the table, who was shocked at how Ignacio ate: "Amazing! What an appetite you have, Ignacio!"

"No – don't you believe it. These are just snacks – just little snacks. Because to eat – to eat the way I eat – I don't dare do it outside of my house."

"Why's that?"

"Well you see, I suffer from a pain, and I can only have it cured at home. Because at home, I'll eat a pot of beans – you see? – if the pain starts, my son José knows how bad it is. He runs and puts a funnel in my mouth, pours in two gallons of water, puts a brush down my throat and scrubs out my stomach.

Whenever you like, I'll challenge him

In the Turisbar there was a time when every morning a Frenchman would show up. He sat at the bar and ordered two fried eggs with fried potatoes and a beer. Then he'd walk around the harbor and he'd show up again a half hour later and order the same thing. By three in the afternoon he'd have eaten six or seven pairs of fried eggs with fried potatoes, and their beers.

One day one of the waiters said to Ignacio: "Shit, Ignacio, this Frenchman shows up here every day at eleven or twelve, and between twelve and three in the afternoon, the guy drinks six or seven beers and eats six or seven pairs of fried eggs with their fried potatoes. I've never seen anyone eat that much in my life!"

And Ignacio: "I can eat more than that, and whenever you like, I'll challenge him. Whoever eats less – whoever gets full first – has to pay."

And that's how it happened: the next day when the Frenchman shows up, they tell him what Ignacio had said, and the foreigner says: "Oh, *oui, oui*! I weel shallange heem when he wants."

They told Ignacio, they introduced them and agreed on a particular night at ten. They agreed to both sit at a table, each ordered whatever they wanted, and whoever got full first would have to pay.

The night arrived; they sat at their table and the waiter said: "You gentlemen tell me what you'd like."

The Frenchman: "I like a halv dozen ov ze zoup of ze shopped meat."

Ignacio jumped in: "Bring me seven!"

"Clo, clo, clo, clo, clo" – they ate up the soup.

"What would you gentlemen like for a second course?"

"I like two kilos ov ze fgied feesh."

"Bring me two and a half kilos!"

They ate and ate and ate and ate ...

"And for a third course?"

"I want halv dozen ov ze fgied boeuf steak."

"Bring me seven!"

You should've seen it – the two of them couldn't stand any more, and us waiting to see who'd bring the cat to the water. The waiter came to take dessert orders, and the Frenchman: "I want a can of queence meat."

The waiter looked at Ignacio – he calmly said: "Bring me a basket of prickly pears."

When he said that, the Frenchman jumped up:

"No more! I pay!"
And we were all yelling: "*Ole! Viva Ignacio!*"
He'd won the challenge.

Ignacio was the laziest man in the world

When Ignacio was fired from the slaughterhouse, he got a recommendation and landed a job as a guard in the park. He talked to the head of the park service and he said: "Look, Ignacio, I'll make you a guard and you won't have to do anything – just sit on a bench and make sure the cats don't go into the gardens."

So as not to have to move from the bench, Ignacio made a whip twenty meters long. If a cat came, he'd scare it with the whip; but nothing got him off that bench.

Except ...

There was a bootblack in Cádiz even lazier than Ignacio. One day, walking across the Plaza San Antonio, Ignacio said to the bootblack: "Hey, what's up, *compadre*? How's work?"

"Work? Very bad. If I get any more, I'll have to hire a kid to carry my box!"

"OK *compadre* – give my shoes a little shine."

The bootblack put the box on the ground so Ignacio could put his foot up, and started shining it. But two minutes later – you better believe it – he heard snoring; Ignacio had fallen asleep. So the bootblack put down his brush, lay his head on Ignacio's knee, and went to sleep too.

What a case!

Thirty nine thousand duros in pin money

There was a *señorito* in Cádiz who would sit in La Habana and drink fourteen or fifteen espressos. One day, while I was there with Ignacio, I ran into him there very pale.

"Pericón, Periconcillo – sit down."

"Whatever you say, don Fernando."

"Pericón, did you hear that the *Marqués* of Camillas died? The poor soul – he called me "son" and I called him "father"! He was the richest man Spain has known – in fact the richest man in the world."

When Espeleta heard that, without knowing anything about the guy, he came out and said: "Listen my friend – what you're saying is a lie!"

My face turned red, but don Fernando said: "What do you mean? I'm lying?"

"Well – I'm not saying it is true or a lie, except the part about him being the richest man in the world ..."

"Ah no? Why do you say he isn't?"

"Well look, I have a friend who has to be richer than the late *Marqués* of Camillas."

"Really? And what assets does this friend of yours have?"

"Look, I don't know what assets he has; what I do know is that every day he gives his wife thirty nine thousand *duros* in pin money."

Thirty nine thousand *duros* in pin money!

I'm here to raffle off this goat

There was a singer in Cádiz that fell ill, and his father – a little tiny thin man – did a penance where he wouldn't shave until his son got better. His son was sick for more than five years.

Because of this, all the artists in Cádiz got together to

put on a benefit so the poor old guy could recoup some of his expenses. We decided to do it in the theater in San José, and while planning it, someone had an idea: "Ignacio Espeleta should be the M.C."

When it was time for the benefit, the theater was packed, everyone was waiting and rambunctious. We told Ignacio: "Come on Ignacio, it's time. Go out with the poor kid's father and thank the public."

The father – so tiny – with that beard that reached his knees – came out with Ignacio, with his huge body next to him.

"Ladies and Gentlemen, Ladies and Gentlemen, I'm here ... I'm here to raffle off this goat."

Of course, when he said that about the goat, there was such a scandal – such a scandal!

With this can of tar

One night Ignacio was in a *fiesta* with a short fat guy whose wife had just died. The guy was in mourning, dressed all black – his pants, shirt, even his collar and beret were black. Well, things happen, and the guy ran out of money – when it came time to pay Ignacio, there wasn't any left.

"I need to give you a present, Igancio."

"Don't worry about it – give it to me tomorrow or the next day."

"No – you're not going home without your present. I don't have anything now, but in a little bit, when the Primera de Cádiz opens, they'll give me what I want and you'll have your present."

"OK, whatever you say."

So they went to the Primera de Cádiz and waited for it to open. Both of them in the doorway, Ignacio, huge, and the other one next to him, tiny, but fat, all dressed in black, with his hands in his pockets and the beret pulled down, waiting for the bank to open. People were walking by, on their way to work. One of them stopped and said to Ignacio: "Ignacio! Why are you standing there like that?"

"Can't you see? I'm here taking care of this can of tar."

El Río de las Ratas

When Franco and Rada and those guys went to Río de la Plata they organized a *fiesta* in Sevilla in the Club Joselito.[44] Sánchez Mejías brought Morcilla and Espeleta to sing.

They were at the banquet, celebrating the occasion, where Espeleta sat down next to a colonel, who kept staring at him, as if to say "who the Hell is this Gypsy?" And the Gypsy – you should have seen – he ate three plates of rice ... The colonel kept looking and looking. Then the speeches started: first a commander of the Air Force, then a colonel, and when several had spoken, Sánchez Mejías and his friends started chanting"

"Let Espeleta speak!"

"We want Ignacio!"

"Ignacio Espeleta should speak!"

"Ignacio Espeleta from Cádiz!"

So Espeleta got up to make his speech – the colonel was looking him up and down – but Ignacio started: "*Señores*, let us not forget the year 1492 when Columbus discovered America."

And the colonel: "This guy's a real talent."

---

[44] The Club Joselito was a major club dedicated to bullfighting in Sevilla. The references to Franco and Rada are to Francisco Franco's brother, the aviator Ramón Franco who in 1926, with a team that included his mechanic Pablo Rada, successfully flew the hydroplane *Plus Ultra* across the Atlantic from Southern Spain (Palos, Huelva) to South America, stopping in the Canaries, Cape Verde, Brazil, Uruguay, and finally, Buenos Aires, Argentina (on the Río de la Plata).

And Espeleta continued: "And today, Spain enjoys the greatest riches: aviation! The whole world envies us because Franco and his companions have made it to the *Río de las Ratas*!"

Río de las Ratas!

And the colonel was ready to hit him: "You shameless idiot! *Río de la Plata!*"[45]

What a scandal!

... *Macandé*

Macandé was a little Gypsy in Cádiz with a voice and an *eco* that I never heard in anyone else. Also, so small and slight and so dark, when he came out with that sound, people said "where does that Gypsy's voice come from?" He never got hoarse – he could sing for twenty hours in a *fiesta*, leave, be called for another, and calmly sang again as if he were fresh.

He and I got along very well, as we were the same age and we were both crazy about the *cante* – we were always in the same places, looking for *juergas* and talking each other each other up.[46] I remember he was always trying to get me to come over to his house for rice and beans. I was always sorry to say no, until one day when his brother had arrived from Buenos Aires – a dancer called el Feo de Cádiz. To celebrate they had organized a *fiesta*. That is when I met Macandé's

---

[45] Espeleta's malapropism confuses *Río de la Plata* 'River of Silver' (so named because it was, in colonial times, a major conduit for Bolivian silver to the Argentinean Atlantic port, then to Spain) with *Río de las Ratas* 'River of Rats'.

[46] Cobo Guzmán (1977) disputes some of the material in these stories – in particular, he claims that Macandé was reclusive and would not have spent much time with Pericón. He also documents Macandé's illness from an early age, suggesting it was not a reaction to his deaf children.

mother.

His mother was just like him – a tiny little Gypsy – but you should have seen her dance with el Feo! And el Feo, how he could play castanets! He closed his eyes and it seemed impossible that someone with two hands could do what he did – and he was a magnificent dancer! But, of course, in the ambience of the *fiestas*, there was little need for dancers, so he had to go to Buenos Aires.

And the rice! It had this and that – rice with beans and fennel – I'll never forget how delicious it was.

So, because of this and that, we got along great, and between the *fiestas* and the coaches, we always ended up together in the mornings.

A fiesta in the 606

The 606 was an establishment without private rooms – just a big salon, and that's where this *fiesta* took place. It turned out that the owner had invited one of his brothers from the mountain to spend some time in Cádiz, and he called us to sing flamenco. The *fiesta* started and the brother – the poor guy was a real brute – took a real liking to me, but hated Macandé. Habichuela was playing guitar, and if I sang, the *Montañés* pricked up his ears, in love with life. But if Macandé sang, this guy acted like jerk and didn't let him sing. This happened over and over again, with Macandé not able to even open his mouth. Until he finally got fed up, went to the bathroom, and there, shut in, in the same key that Habichuela was playing in, started singing with that amazing voice. There he sang as long as he wanted; the *Montañés* trying to open the door, and him singing, without paying any attention, until he was done. When he finally came out, he had to leave, because the *Montañés'* attitude was so bad, not letting him sing. Then we went to the Valdepeñera, and no one sang but him. We drank six or eight bottles of wine, enchanted with Macandé's *cante*. All his things – because everything he sang, he did in his own way – he gave his special touch, that didn't sound like anyone else. To see that little tiny Gypsy with that voice, you were left wondering, "My God, how is this possible?"

When he sang *bulerías*, it was to die. He took the short verses and without losing the rhythm, he broke them up and added things that made them greater than they were – it was barbaric! And all the more with him being so tiny, doing such great things. I'll always remember a verse he sang for *bulerías* that said:

Yo le pido a Dios llorando	Crying, I ask God
que me quite la salú	that He take my health away
y a ti te la vaya dando.	and give it to you.

But such is life; people didn't appreciate what he did, and the poor guy had to work selling candies. With the *fiestas*, he didn't make enough to live. He left in the morning with his tray of candy. To sell them, he made up a *pregón* that mentioned all the bullfighters in Spain.[47] And with that *pregón*, with an *austurianas* melody, all of Cádiz was crazy about him. Wherever he was, there were always thirty or forty people trailing him, just to hear the *pregón*.

And selling candy, he met his wife – the Mute. He married her and then had three kids – all deaf-mute. It was because of that that the poor guy went crazy. They put him in Capuchinos, and there he had a horrible time until he died. He wasn't dangerous or anything; he never hurt anyone. It's just that the deaf kids twisted him in such a way, and he couldn't stand it. I was always with him, and never saw him as

---

[47] This *pregón* is still widely sung today. There are a number of recordings – perhaps most importantly, one by Jose de los Reyes ,"El Negro del Puerto", a friend and contemporary of Macandé's, who recorded it on D-10.

dangerous – just a nervousness that didn't leave him in peace. He would sit down to sing, then get up suddenly and go outside to look at the sky – eccentricities like that, but never bothering anyone.

There in Capuchinos he lived the rest of his life. Caracol went there once with Lola Flores to hear him sing – how they cried listening to Macandé's *fandangos*.

I remember one year they brought him out during Holy Week to sing *saetas*. Andrés Mayo, a great *aficionado*, was a brother in the Cofradía del Cristo del Perdón.[48] Since this Andrés Mayo had a house on Campo del Sur, next to Capuchinos, and knew the director of the asylum, when Holy Week came around, he said: "Hey Antonio, could you let me have Macandé when the Christ stops outside my balcony, so he can sing a *saeta*?"

And since he wasn't dangerous, they let him out with two orderlies. They brought him to Andrés Mayo's house, and when the Christ stopped, Macandé was there waiting to sing. You should have seen – all of Cádiz was waiting outside, because the word got around: "Macandé is going to sing at Andrés Mayo's house."

"Andrés Mayo asked the director to let Macandé out to sing *saetas* to the Cristo del Perdón."

"Macandé is out of Capuchinos to sing *saetas* in Andrés Mayo's house."

" Andrés Mayo ..."

In all, a huge to-do.

The Christ was stopped there, the people waiting, and

---

[48] A *cofradía* is a religious brotherhood organized around a particular saint, Virgin, or Christ, with the purpose of directing Holy Week and other processions. In this case, the Cristo del Perdón, a statue of Christ on the cross, forgiving the thief Dimas, was housed in the Parroquia de Santa Cruz, near the Campo del Sur. The original statue was destroyed in a fire in 1936, and was replaced after the Civil War.

Macandé came out with the two orderlies. Andrés Mayo said "go on, Macandé."

And that Gypsy came out singing *saetas* that gave you shivers. Everyone was silent, with just the sound of the sea, the Christ, and Macandé on the balcony, with that face and that voice:

Tú, que eres Pare de almas,	You, who are the Father of souls,
Ministro de Cristo,	minister of Christ,
Tronco de la Santa Madre Iglesia	trunk of the Holy Mother Church,
y Árbol del Paraíso...	and the Tree of Paradise...

And since the Lord was so close to him, once, without noticing, he touched Christ's face by accident. When Christ swayed, you should have seen: "He told him 'yes'!"

"Christ said 'yes' to Macandé!"

"Macandé – Christ said 'yes' to him!"

... Capinetti

Capinetti was a guitarist in Cádiz who played *soleá* like no one I've ever heard – he had his own *aire* and music ... Then he sang with a falsetto voice that was scary. He sang the double *malagueña* de Mellizo in such a precious way that it made you emotional just hearing it, with that voice and feeling. When he played, he had a lot of things from the Maestro Patiño.

It was the same thing as with Paco Molina, who wasn't a professional guitarist, but took your breath away playing the things of Maestro Patiño. This Paco Molina was in charge of livestock for the Transatlantic Company and never played for anybody. When his ship docked in Cádiz, he'd go to La Habana and sit there and play all by himself.

El Niño de Huelva also played a lot of Patiño's

material, because Patiño was really something – as long as there is guitar, his name will be remembered. And he did it all with a sorry little guitar.[49] But the best guitarist in the world couldn't get the better of him, the way he caressed the strings and the sound he coaxed out of them.

Capinetti played with a rhythm and a meter that was incredible. Aurelio didn't want to sing with anyone else – whenever he had to use another guitarist, things didn't go right. When he was in Cádiz, it was always Capinetti; when he went to Córdoba or Jerez, or someplace like that, he brought Capinetti with him. Only in Sevilla, because Niño de Huelva was there, did Aurelio feel comfortable without him.

And since Capinetti lived only from the guitar and was always thinking about the guitar, sometimes things would happen...

One night we were in the Privaílla – a dancer called el Chino, Capinetti, and me – all of us starving, without a *duro* in our pockets – four or five days without anything. Then around twelve thirty, when Antonio had the lock out and was getting ready to close, the phone rang. Antonio put down the lock and answered: "Yes – this is La Privaílla. Capinetti? Sure – he's here? Pericón and el Chino? Yeah, they're here too – all three of them."

He came over and said to Capinetti, "Here take this call – it's for a *juerga*." Capinetti takes the receiver and says, "Of course, right away – all three of us will be there."

He put down the phone, we go outside, Antonio closes up, and the three of us walk down Benjumeda street. When we got to the corner of Soledad Street, Capinetti stopped short, put

---

[49] Patiño's life spanned the 19th century; hence, his career must have begun before the guitar building innovations of Antonio Torres Jurado (1817-1892), who, in the mid-19th century, is credited with popularizing what is now the standard modern classical guitar. Before Torres, guitars were generally smaller.

down his guitar and said: "Wait! Wait a minute! I don't know where we're going, nor who I talked to!"

"But didn't you just talk to him on the phone?"

"Sure, but I forgot to ask who it was or where it was!"

"Man, Capinetti! This kind of thing only happens to you!"

He made us go through a huge to-do – we got on the phone and called here, there, everywhere – nowhere was there a *fiesta*. So we lost the work because Capinetti couldn't take a message right – he didn't think to say "O.K. – where are we going and what is your name?" Nothing! He didn't ask them anything! We lost the *fiesta* after four or five days without a *peseta*, all of us starving.

It's that he only lived for the guitar – he was a phenomenal guitarist, but the rest...

In lots of *fiestas* with Aurelio, if Aurelio didn't know the *señorito*, he would make up a bogus story to try to get paid forty instead of twenty. He'd say something like: "Listen, it was only four days ago when I was in Córdoba, and so-and-so calls me, and we spent two days at his ranch, and he was really good to us – REALLY good – he paid us very well!"

Aurelio then named an amount so that the *señorito* got the idea. But since Capinetti was right there listening, he would jump in: "What are you talking about? We haven't been to Córdoba in at least three months."

Aurelio kicked him under table so he would take it back, but instead of taking it back, "Stop it! Why are you kicking me? You're dirtying my shoes and pant leg."

But he did it all innocently, without trying to be funny or hurt anyone – what a case!

... *Chiclanita*

When I was young there was a little old man – very tiny, with the same body as Macandé. Since we were such good friends, we were together – either in a *fiesta* or fishing.[50] Back then, I always had salted shrimp meat at home, and Chiclanita often came looking for me to go night fishing. So we went out with our fishing poles, and I had to bring back something because my mother-in-law was waiting – even if I didn't catch anything, on the way home I stopped at a fish stall, so as to not have to hear about it.

I can't even remember all the times I was in *fiesta* with Chiclanita – I really like the way he sang – I learned his *cantes* and then did them my own way. I remember he sang a *romera* with the verse that said:

Baluarte invencible,	Invincible fortress,
Isla de Leon,	Island of Leon,
donde se rindió el coloso	where the colossal
Napoleón Bonaparte	Napoleon Bonaparte surrendered.
y allí perdió su victoria	There he lost his victory
y en Waterloo...	And in Waterloo....[51]

This was a *cante* that I never heard anyone else sing. The same with his *soleá petenera*, which no one else sang either. Even though I was just a kid, I remember the details of

---

[50] Although only occasionally mentioned in this book, Pericón was an avid fisherman. He is also famous for his "fish stories".

[51] The French siege of Cádiz took place from 1810 until 1812, when the French were forced to withdraw. The fact that Cádiz was able to resist the siege has inspired numerous verses, primarily in the *cante* forms of *alegrías* and other *cantiñas*. The Isla de León was renamed Isla de San Fernando in 1813, after King Fernando VII.

those things that had been sung in an earlier time in Cádiz. That's why I asked him about his *cantes* whenever I could. He'd say: "Listen Pericón, when I'm gone, you'll see – you'll be glad to still hear these *cantes*."

"But dear José, I hear you sing them and I know no one else does."

And sure enough, when I moved to Madrid and recorded them, Pepe el de la Matrona said: "No one but Chiclanita ever sang those *cantes*." [52]

... Rosa la Papera

La Papera was a *Gitana* who sang with an art and a rhythm that was amazing. However, she didn't live from her *cante*, and she didn't like going to *fiestas*. If a good *aficionado* wanted to hear her, they'd send me to her house looking for her. It was really hard to convince her to go: "Look Rosa, this is a very good man, and he'll pay you ten *pesetas*."

Of course, during that time, when some guys gave us a *duro* and good night, ten *pesetas* was a bit of money. I would finally convince her to go to the *fiesta*; when I heard her sing, I'd say "My God, can that woman sing!" She sang with a feeling and a measure that moved you – always with *cantes* from Cádiz – *bulerías* and *cantiñas* – with her own style, that wasn't just learned from this guy or the other guy.

... Castelar's mustache

When the Nationalist Movement was in Cádiz, there was a wise guy who was always making jokes. One day he was in front of the statue of Castelar and said:[53] "Ay, don Emilio, my dear don Emilio, if you were to look up and see what's going

---

[52] Pericón recorded Chiclanita's *romera* and the *soleá petenera* on D-7.

on today!"

Just then a cop happened by and heard. He grabbed him and said: "You – shameless! What were you saying?"

"No – nothing ..."

"What do you mean nothing? I heard it all – let's go!"

So he took him to the police station, and told the commissioner:

"This shameless idiot was in front of the statue of Castelar saying 'if you were to look up and see what's going on today!'"

The commissioner: "So – you're also one of those Commies?"

And the wise guy: "No Sir, Commissioner! I didn't mean anything by it. I was talking about mustaches – that if he were to look up and see all the little mustaches men have today!"

... Antonio Mayo

Antonio Mayo was a practical joker. He liked nothing more than a practical joke and spent days thinking them up.

I remember one thing he did – a really famous incident. He said to his friend: "I'm going to do something no one has ever done before – I'm going to put together something in the Plaza Gaspar del Pino that no one has ever seen."

"What are you going to do?"

"If you want to find out, go by the Plaza Gaspar del Pino at eleven this Saturday morning – you'll see."

And at eleven that Saturday morning, in the Plaza

---

[53] Emilio Castelar y Ripoll (1832-1899) was a Cádiz-born president of Spain's first republic, known for his moderate politics. He had a very large handle-bar mustache. His statue stands in Cádiz in the Plaza de la Candelaria, where he was born. In 1933, for unknown reasons, the statue was knocked off its pedestal and left thrown in the plaza garden.

Gaspar del Pino were all the hunchbacks in Cádiz – all forty or fifty of them. When they saw each other, they started talking:

"Look – City Hall sent me this notice saying to be here at eleven for something important, and that I better be sure to be here."

"Me too – I got the same thing."

Then another and another, until all the hunchbacks were glancing at each other – then twelve o'clock came, then one, and then they decided that there was nothing going on, that it was a joke, and they left.

That's Antonio Mayo and the kinds of things he thought up.

... *Curro Villaescusa*

Curro Villaescusa was a guy with a lot of *ángel* – of course everyone loved him – all the *señoritos* in Cádiz, and all the flamencos appreciated him because he never bothered anyone or criticized anyone. That's why he was always in the *fiestas*, without paying a *peseta*. I remember once I was in La Privaílla with him, when a man came in and told him very seriously.

"Curro do me a favor."

"Whatever you want."

"Curro – do you think this is right – can this be?"

"What's wrong?"

And the guy pulled out a list with at least a hundred names on it, and started to say: "This guy owes me six thousand *pesetas*, this one three thousand five hundred, this other one two thousand three hundred, and this one a thousand two hundred ..."

Curro stood there listening, without saying anything; when he finished with the list, Curro said:

"All right – that's enough! Just give me twenty *duros*

and put me at the end of the list!"

Another time Curro had been in a fiesta with Manuel Camacho, Manolete, and don Manuel. They got in a fight, but then he gave Curro five hundred *pesetas*. He went off to a *venta* with a singer named Ruiseñor – by morning he didn't have even a *duro* left. When the fiesta was over, he said to Ruiseñor: "I'll take care of you tomorrow."

But one day went by, then another, and then fifteen more, and Curro never remembered to pay Ruiseñor. This, until one day they happened to be in La Privaílla together – each sitting opposite the other, Ruiseñor watching him, and Curro moving from one place to another, and Ruiseñor following him. That went on for awhile, from table to table, until Curro started to sing:

A mí me importa poco	What do I care
que un pájaro en la alamea	that a bird on the avenue
se pase de un árbol a otro...	goes from one tree to the next...

That's how Curro Villaescusa went through life.

... Paco Añote

This Paco Aõnte was someone who was always thinking up mischief – funny mischief. One day we were playing *mus*, and he said: "Tonight we're going to a amateur theater production of Don Juan Tenorio."[54]

We went to the theater, which was on Hospital de Mujeres Street – we went in, sat down in the third row, and the show started. The characters started coming on stage: first one,

---

[54] *Don Juan Tenorio: Drama religioso-fantástico en dos partes* ('Don Juan Tenoria: Religio-fantastic drama in two parts') is an 1844 play by José Zorilla, based, in part, on an earlier work by Tirso de Molina.

then another, and when the commander came on – everyone knows that the commander comes on as a statue in the cemetery – the comedian who played the commander was there very serious, acting like a statue, with his hands crossed. Paco Añote took out slingshot, stretched it out, and shot a pebble that hit the commander in the face. Of course since the commander was a statue, he couldn't move; all he could do was grimace. Paco got another pebble and started pulling the sling. The poor commander was scared, looking with his eyes around the room, trying to see who had shot the pebble. When he saw Paco and saw that he was taking aim – my God! – you should have seen his face! Poor guy – he couldn't move, but trying to move his face out of the way. Finally everyone started to laugh and it was a scandal.

Everything he did was like that – the only thing he liked was making mischief.

One year his wife said: "Paco, why don't you take me to see the *puchinelas*?"

The *puchinelas* were marionettes, there was Uncle Batillo, the Tía Nódica, and stuff like that.[55] Paco told her: "Woman, why would I want to do that? They're for little kids."

"Well, all the other husbands are taking their wives to see them."

Of course, she then started in with this and that until she convinced him to take her to see the *puchinelas*. But he thought to himself "I'll take her, but she'll never ask me to do it again." They got to the *puchinelas* at two and sat in the bleachers. When Batillo came on – he was a really bad puppet, who was always bugging the grandmother – Paco Añote started screaming – but really screaming: "Ayyy! I want a Batillito! I

---

[55] The Tía Nódica marionette shows have been popular in Cádiz since the 19th century. They involve an old woman, Tía Nódica, and her grandson, Batillito, who was the model of an ill-behaved boy.

want a Batillitoooo!"
    And everyone looking at them and saying:
    "*Señora*, take that retard out of here!"
    The poor woman: "Paco! God! Paco!"
    But Paco wouldn't stop – acting even more like he was
retarded and screaming louder:"Ayyyy! I want a Batillitoooo!"
    Until his wife, mortified, had to take him out.

... *Lucas el Disparate*

One of the most renowned men in Cádiz during that time was
Lucas el Disparate. He had a bar that was the ultimate in
gracia.   Walking in, you were faced with a wall with the
painting of a man, his eyes popping out, and a bubble with him
saying "Come on rats! Here is the rat-killer!" The guy had rats
all over him – on his shoulders, his head... Then on the same
wall there was another painting with a bullfighter down on all
fours, and a bull standing up with his cape, taking the
bullfighter's charge – everything backwards.
    If you came in and he saw you were new, he would
come up and say, very serious:
    "Listen, if you don't like it down here, why not go
upstairs to the salon – you'll be happier there."
    When you went to go upstairs, you saw that behind a
curtain the stairs were painted on the wall. If you wanted to
make a phone call, he brought out a box, closed with an L-
hook; you took off the hook, and there was a stick inside.
Once you'd seen all of this, and were having a drink, Lucas
came up with those little flea-eyes:
    "Would you like a *tapa*?"
    "Sure – give me a specialty of the house."
    "I could give you some great anchovies."
    "Sounds good."

He went into the kitchen very serious and came out with a plate of L-hooks. If you laughed, he would take away the plate and say: "Well, if you don't like the anchovies, how about some cheese?"

The cheese was a piece of millstone – on top of that, he gave you a knife and said "cut off as much as you like."

That's why he was called Lucas el Disparate.

Two years later, he left the bar and went to Corona – a *venta* outside *Puerta Tierra*. We got together there at night – twelve or fourteen artists – singers, dancers, guitarists – because it was a nice place with Lucas there. This man had the biggest heart I've seen.

He would come in on those winter nights when no one came out for a *fiesta*, us waiting and waiting, until three in the morning. Lucas told the waiter: "Tell the artists to go into one of the rooms, give them four or five bottles of red wine, and tell the cook to fry them some fish."

They gave us our wine and our fish, with bread and olives then at three in the morning – all of us starving, without having earned a *peseta*. But that wasn't all – later he came into the room and said: "*Señores*, excuse me, please accept a *duro* each for groceries."

Because of that, whenever we had a *señorito*, we'd say: "Let's go to Corona – it's great there."

And there we went to give him the business, because he had us all hooked with his heart and his quirks.

Then he had so much *gracia*. Whatever party we came to Corona with, after we'd drunk six or eight bottles of wine, we'd start talking about Lucas' verses, and the things that he came up with. The *señorito* called him and got him to agree to sing a few of his *fandangos* that made you die:

La quería más que ninguna   I loved her more than anything,
a la mujer que yo le hablaba   the woman I just told you about

ahora por último,

La quería más que ninguna,	I loved her more than anything,
y ahora l'aborrecío	and now I hate her
porque no cree en las vacunas	because she doesn't believe in vaccinations,
y está llena salpullíos.	and she's covered with boils.

And then:

Antes que el mal sobrevenga	Before things start going wrong
mujer, te voy a advertir,	I'm warning you, woman,
antes que el mal sobrevenga,	before things start going wrong,
no vayas luego a venir	don't come back later
con las dos piernas abiertas	with your legs spread
pidiéndome el pirulín.	asking for my lollipop.

And they spend some time listening to his verses and with his *disparates*:

A pedirle a Dios cien duros	To ask God for a hundred *duros*
un artista subió al cielo,	an artist went up to heaven
a pedirle a Dios cien duros,	to ask God for a hundred *duros,*
y le contestó San Pedro:	and Saint Peter answered:
«Vaya usté a tomar por culo;	"Go take it up the ass;
aquí no se quieren gamberos».	we don't want bums here."

... María Bastón

María Bastón was an old lady in Cádiz, always very well dressed, always on the street with her cane. If she saw you from the other side of the street, she'd call you: [56]

---

[56] María Bastón is immortalized in a *tanguillo* verse, now sung as a major key *bulerías de Cádiz*; see Translator's Forward.

"Hey! Hey you!"
You'd go over to her.
"What can I do for you, *señora*?"
She'd say, with great formality: "Could you give me a
perra for the trolley?"
You'd give it to her, and off she went with her cane.
Then the next person she saw: "Hey! Hey you!"
That way she spent all day gathering *perras* for the
trolley.

... *El Colorao and Perico el de Las Viejas Ricas*

Among the really funny types in Cádiz, El Colorao and Perico
el de Las Viejas Ricas really took the cake for the things they
thought up – things with real *gracia*. El Colorao was short and
plump, with a red face – that's why they called him *colorao*
('red'). They called Perico *el de Las Viejas Ricas* because he
had performed with a chorus in Carnaval called Las Viejas
Ricas. Of course, since they knew the Cádiz scene and were so
steeped in it, they were always together coming up with stuff.

Oh – skeleton!

Once, when they were both starving, they ran into seven or
eight tourists in the Plaza la Catedral. On seeing them, El
Colorao said to Perico: "Hey man, we can earn some money
there."
"How?"
"Don't be funny! Man – being a guide! You go over and
say you're the best guide in Cádiz, then you show them

whatever they want to see."

"Why don't you do it?"

"Because I don't have the gift of gab, but you do."

Since they were both broke and hungry, Perico went over to the tourists and started:

"Cathedral!"

And the tourists:

"Oh – Cathedral. Pretty Cathedral"

"I'm the best guide in Cádiz."

"Oh – best guide in Cádiz – you show Cathedral."

"Right away!"

So they went to the Cathedral. One of the tourists took out a cigarette case and passed out cigarettes to everyone, except Perico – he didn't give him anything. And Perico was dying for a cigarette ...

They went into the Cathedral. As soon as they were inside, they came on an urn with a skeleton in it. Of course, Perico didn't know anything about the skeleton, who it was or anything, but one of the tourists asked:

"Oh – skeleton. Who skeleton?"

"Skeleton? It's the skeleton of the first *Gallego* to come to Cádiz."

"Oh – first *Gallego* who come to Cádiz skeleton!"

They kept going, one room, another, and in the third, they came upon a little urn with a little skeleton. The tourist asked: "Oh – little skeleton! Who little skeleton?"

"Skeleton! It's the skeleton of the first *Gallego* to come to Cádiz."

"Oh – no possible! Big skeleton first *Gallego* in Cádiz and little skeleton first *Gallego* in Cádiz, no possible!"

"By my mother, man! It's from when the *Gallego* was a kid!"

They kept going and the tourist with the cigarette case got more out and passed them around, except not for Perico.

98

They were walking all around, and came to a corner with a lone saint. The tourist asks again:

"Oh – what saint? What name?"

"Saint Anthony!"

"Oh – Saint Anthony no possible!"

"What do you mean – that I can't recognize Saint Anthony?"

"No – no possible – Saint Anthony has a child."

"I know that, wise guy, I know. But I sent the kid out to get me cigarettes."

The escort for Rafael el Gallo

Once, when Rafael el Gallo came from bullfighting in America, Perico el de Las Viejas Ricas saw in the paper that "A certain Rafael el Gallo would arrive from America on a certain Tuesday on a certain boat." Right away it occurred to Perico to make eight straw horses and prepare an escort for el Gallo. He made the horses, and when the day came, he, and seven of his toadies – some of the best known guys in Cádiz – got on them and went to the port to wait for Rafael el Gallo.

Rafael arrived, and when he saw those horses with a sign saying "Rafael el Gallo's Escort," he was so happy to see the *gracia* of Cádiz. He got in his car, and the eight of them ran after it, so as not to lose the tip, to the Hotel Francia. Rafael asked for the leader of the escort, and Perico went up, and in those days – in those days! – Rafael gave him two thousand *pesetas* for the escort. When Perico got back – you should have seen the rest of the escort! Perico took off running, saying "catch me if you can!"

He ran down San Francisco Street, with all the horses chasing him, until he got to the Plaza San Juan de Dios – there he ordered a halt, they dismounted and shared the money.

Mamá caca!

During Carnival time, the things they came up with were out of this world. One year they went out as a nursing baby and a nanny.

El Colorao played the part of the baby, in his carriage, with his baby clothes and baby bottle. Perico el de Las Viejas Ricas played the nanny – dressed like a real nanny. They went around to all the bars begging for wine; every time they passed a bar, El Colorao said to the maid: "*Mamá, caca; Mamá, caca.*"

And then Perico knew El Colorao wanted wine. But one time they ran into a wise guy barman; when El Colorao said that stuff about *caca*, he sent a glass of wine with *jalap*.[57] Two minutes later, you should have seen it -- El Colorao's gut looked like an earthquake, and the poor guy: "*Mamá, caca! Mamá caca!*"

But since Perico didn't know what was going on: "Wait a little son, you just made *caca*."

And El Colorao, not able to stand it:

"Mamá! Mommy! This is real *caca*!"

They had to take off running, with the carriage full of real *caca*.

Doltol X

Another year they went out playing Doltol X and a sick lady. First Perico el de Las Viejas Ricas went out with a mule cart, with railings and a table in the middle, covered with tools and a little bell. He was dressed as Doltol X – with a top hat, a long, fake beard, and black livery. When he arrived somewhere with a crowd, he started ringing his bell, started talking with a

---

[57] *Jalap* is a root used in medicine as a cathartic, purging agent.

French accent: "Glspecteeble poobleek, Glspecteeble poobleek! Fol ze feelst time een Spain ze Doltol X – ze Doltol X comes to cure all ze seeckness – howevel bad. And I cure zem een five minute! Are zel señoges flom ze publeek zat haf a pain? Whatevel eet ees, ze Doltol X make eet gude.

Then the crowd heard a yell: "Ay, ayy, ayyy, what horrible pains I have!"

It was El Colorao, dressed as an old lady, with his hands on his chest braying. When Doltol X saw him, he said: "Let hel srough; let zees poor old lady srough!"

The old lady got up, acting like she could barely do it because of her horrible pains. When she got up finally, she sat down, and he began to examine her: "What eez glong, señoga?"

And El Colorao screaming – but really screaming: "Ayyyyy, what pains have I!"

"And whege dos eet hult, *señoga*?"

"Right here in the jaw!"

"Ah – zat eez nothing. Eet eez only a bad toos, señoga – I gleemove eet glight away!"

Doltol X threw a cloth on her head, and took a pair of pliers, like those for removing stitches, with everyone watching. The doctor pulled and pulled; the lady screaming and screaming, until the doctor said: "Quiet *señoga*, heer eez ze ploblem, and now you'g fine!"

Saying that, he pulled out from under the cloth a huge donkey bone, and the poor lady sweating.

"Ay doltol, ay doltol! How relieved I am, how relieved!"

Of course, the people gave them something for their performance. Later they picked up and left – Perico with the cart and El Colorao with his donkey bone, to later meet up again at a bar door. That way, night and day, and they split the take that evening.

101

... *El Magaña*

There was a famous character in Cádiz called el Magaña. He was sitting with us in the Plaza San Juan de Dios when he said "Tomorrow I'm going to Havana." We thought he was joking, but the next day, when we didn't see him, nor the next, nor the next, we were convinced that he had really gone to Havana. He would leave, spend six or seven months there, and once he had accumulated enough money, he'd come back to Cádiz to spend it. He'd spend it and once he was left without tobacco again, he'd stow away in a boat bound for Buenos Aires or Havana.

During his last trip he was away at least three or four years: Puerto Rico, Veracruz, Havana, New York, all of those places, making money to later throw it away in Cádiz. He'd arrive in Cádiz in style: ten or twelve expensive suits, three or four coats, rings, a gold watch, all in all well off. On top of that, with fresh money, when the people in Cádiz found out he was back: "Magaña's back."

"Magaña is back with a gold watch."

"You should see the rings Magaña's got."

"Magaña brought fifteen suits."

And Magaña was spending money – every night a *juerga*, *cante*, wine, calling singers ... One of his favorites was Cojo Peroche, because he loved how he danced and sang. One night in this place, the next in another place ... until after seven or eight nights Magaña got tired of Cojo Peroche, and stopped calling him. At this point, Magaña was selling off his stuff; he'd sold the watch, the rings, the coats, and now was starting in on the suits. Of course Peroche's friends, knowing they had had a falling out, went around saying: "Magaña sold his watch."

"Last night Magaña sold a suit and went to a *juerga*."

"This morning Magaña sold another suit to pay for a *fiesta.*"

And Peroche, upset that he wasn't called, said: "Oh forget about it! I only see him like the ghost of the Viña, with a sheet on his head."

There was a time when a ghost came out in the barrio de la Viña every night. At least that's what people said. There was a big scandal every night around ten, because someone would get the idea to say "There's the ghost!" – and then it was a big mess – everyone ran out to their balconies, the women screaming, and everyone saying what they thought they saw: "Look! It's on that roof!"

"I saw it on the corner there!"

"Just a minute ago it was right there!"

The police showed up, the *serenos*, but no one caught it. Three or four days went by, and everyone had forgotten about it, until some wise guy piped up "Look at it! Look at it!" Then the scandal all over again, without there really being a ghost or anything. Later, at Carnival time, they made up a song making fun of the ghost:

En el barrio de la Viña	In the barrio de la Viña
hace ya días	a few days ago
que sentimos una noche	we heard one night
gran gritería:	a big cry:
una vieja fue la causa	an old lady was the source
de aquel montín,	of that to-do
porque vio que la fansatma	because she saw that the ghost
estaba subía arriba el pretil.	was up on the balcony.
A los gritos acudieron	The shouts brought in
cuarenta serenos y un municipal,	forty *serenos,* and a city cop,
catorce carabineros, siete vigilantes	fourteen guards, seven vigilantes

y un cabo de mar.	and a ship captain.
Cuando subieron arriba,	When they all climbed up,
lo que s'encontraron,	what they found,
* poner atención:*	pay attention:
unos calzoncillos blancos	A pair of white underwear
y un cacharro de almidón,	and a pot of starch,
y el gato de la casera	and the house cat
dando volteras	doing somersaults
dento de un perol.	inside of a pot.

... *El Nene*

There was a *Gitano* in Cádiz called el Nene who had a phenomenal *ángel*. The poor guy survived by selling this and that, but what he sold most often were hazelnuts at the bull fights. One year, close to Corpus Christi, a *señorito* friend of his said: "Nene, why don't you set up your hazelnut stand in Plaza San Juan de Dios for Corpus Christi?"

"Son of my soul!" said Nene "I'm going to set up six kilos of hazelnuts? For me to put up a whole sack of nuts, prepared ...?"

"How much would that run?"

"Well each sack is fifteen *duros*."

So, he gave him the money, and Nene did his part and went to the City Hall to get the license; then he set up his stand in Plaza San Juan de Dios.

But after awhile, singing his *pregón* to sell the hazelnuts, someone began to put up a big stand right next to his. Nene was thinking "what are they putting up there?" Finally they finished and it was a tooth extractor – one who spoke half French and half Spanish: "*Señoges*, if zer ees someone wis a bad toos, come up and I pool eet immediately, wisout pain and wisout costing a cent!"

Of course, someone with a bad tooth: "Let's see! I'll

take advantage of this."

And Nene next door, with his little voice: "Hazelnuts, hazelnuts, hazel nuuuuuts."

That's how he was for hours, without selling a single hazelnut, while the tooth puller already had twelve or fourteen pulled. Of course he was mad. He packed up the stand, emptied the hazelnuts into their bag, and went to City Hall to look for the assistant mayor. He demanded to see the assistant mayor, and since he was so funny and knew everyone, they let him through right away: "So, Nene, what's the problem – what do you want?"

"What do I want? That you give me back my money for the license! You sent me there, then next to me there was a tooth extractor, and the people only wanted to have teeth pulled. And me next to this, trying to sell hazelnuts, without selling a single one, because, you see, who's going to buy hazelnuts after having their teeth pulled? How will they crack them?"

... *Macanudo and el Ñoñi*

There was a guitarist, Servando Roa, who would do anything to earn a *peseta*. Since he was out and about, he knew a lot of people and got along with them. I remember one of the *fiestas* that we had with Bolo, a guy who rented the bullring to put on young bulls and things like that. We were in a *fiesta*, when Bolo said to Servando: "Hey Servando, let's see if you can find me three or four low-lifes from Cádiz to put on a show with guys like that and young bulls."

"I'll take care of it," said Servando. "Don't worry – I'll take care of everything."

Then they went looking for Macanudo. Macanudo was a *Gallego*, very short, and really funny, who worked as a street cleaner. Servando was kissing up – this, that, and the other thing. Finally, Macanudo said:

"But I've never fought a bull in my life!"

"Don't worry, Macanudo. Don't worry because they'll give you a little bull – anyone could kill it."

That way, we convinced him to go, and he started looking up low-lifes for the group. There was Gaditanito, who was more afraid than funny – and with him being so funny. The son of the Maestro Pulpo ('octopus') – he was over thirty, but they still called him by his father's name, because he went to Caleta to catch octopi. And then another called Mojama.

They all signed the contracts, and the day of the bullfight approached. But the impresario, Bulo, didn't trust Macanudo, so to feel more secure, he said to Servando: "Look Servando, I'm not sure Macanudo is going to show up."

"No, man, don't worry don Miguel. I promise you that Macanudo will fight those bulls. I just have to tell him to fight them, and he'll fight them – I promise."

"All right, but the only thing is that since the show is Saturday, I want Macanudo here at the bullring Friday morning."

So Friday morning they went and got Macanudo and brought him to the bullring. They put him in a horse stall, and there he stayed, waiting for the bullfight. When it started – you should have seen – Macanudo, so little, dressed as a bullfighter, doing the passes... The people died laughing just seeing him, because he came out making these faces and stuff from the fleas he had picked up in the horse stall – the poor guy came out covered in fleas – and scratched and scratched.

Then when things got under way, it was to die. The bull ran around fifty times. Gaditanito ran and hid at the sight of it. Macanudo came out with a cigar in his mouth and tried to kill the bull with the scabbard ... All funny things that they did without rehearsing, because it just came out that way.

They gave Macanudo the ears, because they always

gave the ears. He kept them in a shoebox, in salt, to take them back to his homeland, so people would see that they presented him with ears in Cádiz.

Later on they had other shows. There was a Mexican named Rosember, who inserted the *bandarillas* with his mouth. You should have seen what a scandal! Everyone was crazy about him – the bullring was packed every time he was came out to put in the *banderillas* with his mouth – what a case! Then there was a wise guy in Cádiz – he was called El Ñoñi – a hotel guide. He went to Bolo and said: "I can put in the *banderillas* with my mouth like Rosember does."

"OK – how much do you want?"

"Three thousand *pesetas* not a penny less. Furthermore, I'll put them in with my hands tied behind my back – no hands."

Of course, Bolo was thinking "this will fill the bullring – when I announce El Ñoñi – so well-known around here – is going to put in the *banderillas* with his mouth with his hands tied ..."

"OK - Ñoñi, whatever you say."

So that was it – he got everything ready, put up posters all over Cádiz, hired two or three more low-lifes to fill things out, and when the time came, you should have seen – the bullring full – everyone waiting for El Ñoñi: "Ñoñi! Ñoñi!"

El Ñoñi came out with the *banderillas* in his mouth, stuck into a piece of cork, his hands tied, just as he said, and went out to the middle of the ring to wait for the bull.

The bull came out, came after Ñoñi, Ñoñi watching it, then he broke to one side, but the bull turned the other way, and look – it looked like someone had broken a string of pearls – teeth and molars flying all over.

He was a month recovering, but he'd done it. He'd put in the *banderillas* with his mouth. Not a tooth in his head, but he'd done it. And it made him really famous; everywhere, on

the street: "El Ñoñi."
   "Look – El Ñoñi."
   "Look, there goes El Ñoñi."
   "El Ñoñi."

... The Macho of the Viña

In Cádiz there was a woman called the Macho of the Viña. She was a lesbian who lived in the barrio de la Viña, whose name was Amalia Ponce de León Atorruyos y Rivas. This woman was a case: she lived with her girlfriend and she went out to earn a living just like she was a regular guy; everything she earned was for the house, her girlfriend, and for her.

I remember one night there was a *fiesta* in the Tres Reyes. In the *fiesta* was a guy named Camacho Ortiz, from Puerto Santa María, who exported English roosters to Havana, and who sang with a wonderful *ángel*. Also there was Pastorín, who was a grocery merchant, Servando Rava, a butcher, and the artists were Diego Antúnez, Antonio el Mellizo, el Morcilla, and Pericón – that is, me. I remember it being a night of a lot of *gracia*.

At one point Antonio el Mellizo got together with Pastorín singing opera. Antonio sang, while Pastorín played the violin, on a ham he'd grabbed from the kitchen. Antonio sang: *La donna inmóbili*, while Pastorín played the ham with a knife, cutting off huge pieces. The owner of the Tres Reyes said: "*Piano*, Pastorín, *piano*," so that he's cut smaller pieces. Finally, around six in the morning, when we'd eaten and everything, the Macho de la Viña came by earning her living – the poor thing begged for a *peseta*. Since we all knew her, one gave her a *peseta*, another two, and the leftovers on the table, she started grabbing – you should have seen, she stuffed herself and drank all she could, and then stuffed as much as she could in her shirt. But with all the wine she'd drunk, she was soused, and fell asleep in the doorway of Tres Reyes.

The poor thing was there asleep in the doorway, when a guy called el Puchi came by – someone who sold carnations and flowers – Puchi saw her with her shirt stuffed, and started shaking her saying:

"Look – daughter of the Great Whore – with your breast stuffed with bread – we're going to the scales – to the scales!"

Because then in Cádiz, there were bread scales, where you'd take a basket of bread to be weighed, and if it came short, the baker was fined, and the bread was given to charity. Puchi grabbed the Macho de la Viña and put her in a cart he had and wheeled her inside, yelling "to the scales! to the scales!"

And poor Amalia, now awake: "Son of the Great Whore, Puchi, I shit in your mother's milk, let me out or I'll pee on you!"

It's that Amalia, when she was drunk, was a real demon from Hell; she'd get mad at anyone, and when they least expected it, she'd lift her skirt and start peeing on them, just like a guy. She grabbed her parts, and could pee farther than a guy – poor thing.

... La Zubiela

La Zubiela was a famous *maricón* in Cádiz – a *maricón* from birth, with no way to change it. He was effeminate in such a way that he really seemed like a woman. He was the prettiest man I've ever seen, with such style dressing – his brown suit, his wide-brimmed hat, also brown, his brown shoes. What a case – a guy, who despite being Gay, had lots of women crazy about him, because he was so funny and pretty.

Once he was hooked up with someone who gave him a disease, so he went to the doctor. He went to the office, they had him pull down his pants, and when he had his butt in the air, the doctor said: "It seems that something has been in here."

"What do you mean something? There's been sack races through there!"

That's just the type of *gracia* he had – with everything that happened to him.

Once in Barcelona – he went to work as a performer in the Café Borrull, singing and dancing with an incredible *ángel* – the Nationalist Movement picked him up. This was because the poor guy was starving, without earning a *peseta*, and every morning he went to a butcher friend to get something to eat, but no way – the butcher didn't give him anything. Finally, one day, so he wouldn't come back, the butcher gave him a sheep's head, but it was really empty, wrapped up in paper so he wouldn't notice right away. You should have seen Zubiela leaving, thinking he really had some meat. He ran to his house and unwrapped the package. After cursing the butcher, he went back to the stand and said in a clear voice: "Take this and I hope you get stabbed ten times! Take this and save it for when they gas you!"

Another time, after the war, he was also broke, and Juanito Valderrama came to Barcelona. When Zubiela realized, he went to the theater to try to get something out of him. He went to the stage door and said to the porter: "Oh, please, my dear, let me in – I need to tell Juanito something!"

And the porter, very serious: "You can't come in – no one is allowed in."

"What? Not even me, Zubilea?"

"No – no one – Juanito said that no one is allowed in."

Zubiela saw there was no way, so he said: "Well look, son, don't you think I'm here to try to get something out of Juanito. It's that tomorrow, I'm leaving for China, and I just want to see if he has anything he wants me to say to his family."

What genius! Since Juanito Valderrama had Chinese-looking eyes, he came up with that for the porter.

Wherever he went, he took that wonderful *gracia*, and became famous. When he worked in Barcelona, all the aristocrats were crazy about him.

Later, when other *maricones* come out, when asked where they are from, they say they're from Cádiz. That's because of the fame he acquired with his ways and sayings – everyone wanted to be like him. Without being from Cádiz at all, they still said they were from Cádiz.[58]

The poor guy's name was José.

---

[58] Cádiz has a reputation for its Gay population. This is commented on in popular stories, as well as in literature, such as Genet's *Our Lady of the Flowers*.

3. WHERE, O DEATH, IS THY VICTORY?

The Big One

One year the big lottery prize was won by a dancer called Juan el Churri and a musician.

On the day of the drawing there was a fancy funeral that had music for the corpse. They all assembled: the hearse with its horses, the corpse, the staff, and the band playing. And this musician is playing saxophone in the band – he played and played, until the procession passed down Compañia Street, and went by a Lottery office. The musician snuck a look at the board where the winning numbers were posted, and saw his number winning the Big One.

You should have seen what he did! He stood there playing his sax at the number while the funeral procession moved on, but him standing still playing to the number. In a little while Juan el Churri came by with his winning ticket and found the musician.

You should have seen it – the musician playing and Juan dancing to the funeral music.

The number was 11.013

Bullfight Tickets

In Cádiz there once was a *Gitano* named Curro. Whenever he was out with his wife, he was well-dressed: his short suit, his vest, his *Calañés* hat, his walking stick, his gold chain ...

This guy never went anywhere alone – he was about 75 or 76 years old – he was always with his wife. And he was terrified of death. Whenever he spoke with his wife – if he was feeling ill – he'd say: "Lola – my Lola! If I die before you, I want you to have me buried just as I am; just put me in the box the way I am."

"Stop it! Don't worry! But, Curro, stop saying these things."

They'd always have this argument. Such is life; Curro eventually died, and the poor *Gitana*, since they'd had that discussion so many times about burying him as he was, said to her friends, when they came to help: "Don't touch him! Don't touch my Curro – I'll embalm him myself; I'll fix him up the way he told me to so many times."

You should have seen; she dressed him in his short suit, his vest, his Calañés hat, his walking stick, his gold chain ...

Curro was there in the coffin when La Zubiela came in crying – he'd loved Curro so much.[59]   Lola got up and said: "Oh Zubiela! Look at my poor Curro – my poor Curro, who always asked me to embalm him as he was – they way he always dressed when we went out. There he is; you know him, did I do it right? Is there anything missing?"

La Zubiela looked into the coffin and said: "No Lola – it's fine, very good. Nothing is missing – nothing except bullfight tickets!"[60]

Does he think he's a sailboat?

In the barrio Santa María lived a *Gitana* who really loved her husband.   But the poor guy contracted tuberculosis, or something like that, and was failing ... This Gitana, cried all day: "Ay! Dear Curro of my soul, my poor Curro!"

And the neighbors: "How is Curro doing?"

---

[59] See Part 2, "La Zubiela".

[60] The connotation is that he is "all dressed up with nowhere to go".

"I don't know. The doctor said he's a little better – we'll see. Oh, God save him. If my Curro were to die, I don't know – I'd jump off a roof!"

She was like that every day with the neighbors. Until one day – the kind of winter's day that takes away many to the other side – the doctor came, and when he came out – poor Curro clearly was on his last legs – he told the *Gitana*: "Listen, I'm afraid he'll go with the tide."

The doctor left, the *Gitana* was crying, and neighbors asking: "What did the doctor say? How did he find Curro?"

"Ay! I don't know! Don José told me that my Curro will go with the tide. But does he think my husband's a sailboat?"

How will I die?

There was a *Gitana* in the barrio Santa María who went to the church every morning when it opened and prayed to the Christ: "My Father! You're so beautiful! Such black eyes, such curls, nothing in the world is as beautiful! Tell me Father, how will I die?"

Of course, the Christ didn't say anything – what was He going to say? Finally, the *Gitana* got tired and stood up: "You won't say, right, Father? All right – I'll see you tomorrow, beautiful."

The next day the same – when the priest opened the church, the *Gitana* was on her knees in front of the statue: "Ay! You're even more beautiful than yesterday. I've never seen a face like yours: that narrow nose, that little mouth; what a beautiful face my Father! Tell me, my Father, how will I die?"

But the Christ still wouldn't say a thing.

"All right – I'll see you tomorrow, beautiful."

It was like that day after day, until one day the priest

thought: "We'll see how after the *Gitana* comes today, she won't come again."

Sure enough, when the *Gitana* arrived that day, kneeling before the statue and starting her routine: "There's no one in the world more beautiful than you. Why won't you tell me how I will die so I can relax?"

And the priest, hiding behind the statue said in a hollow voice: "You'll hang!"

The *Gitana* jumped up and ran for the door, but before she went out, she turned and said: "And who told you that, hawk-face?"

Goodbye cagón!

Once an old man – fiftyish – from Málaga came to Cádiz and put up a shop selling chotskies and stuff like that in barrio Santa María.

And such is life – a young *Gitana* – about eighteen or twenty – came into the shop one day, and he fell in love with her. He was so in love that they got married: she was a young thing at eighteen and he was fifty-something and already old.

Since he was so in love with her, he bought her anything she wanted – she never wanted for a thing: "Ay Manolito, I saw these bracelets!"

Two hours later she had the bracelets.

"Ay Manolito, I saw these earrings!"

Two hours later she had the earrings.

But life happens, and the guy fell ill; every two minutes he'd say to the *Gitana*: "Ay Lolita! Bring me the chamber-pot!"

The poor *Gitana* – eighteen or twenty and having to put the chamber-pot in the bed with her husband trembling like crazy.

"Ay – there – that's it dear."

115

The poor girl took the chamber-pot away, holding her nose. Then five or ten minutes later: "Ay – Lolita – the chamber-pot!"

It went on like that for five or six days until he finally died, completely dehydrated from crapping twenty to thirty times a day. Then at the wake, the poor woman had to pretend that she loved him so much: "Ay, Manolo of my soul – what a horrible death!"

When the time came for the burial, the *Gitana* went crazy: "Let me by! Let me by! I want to say goodbye to my Manolo."

"Girl, there's nothing you can do."

"Leave me alone! I need to say goodbye!"

Until finally: "All right – let her say goodbye."

The hearse was already making its way down Campo del Sur, when the *Gitana* went out on the balcony, looking crazy, and said: "Good bye *cagón!*"

You should have seen the scandal – poor thing...

Baldomero the Gitano

When I was eighteen or nineteen in Cádiz, singing in the coach *fiestas*, I remember how every time the Monserrat came to port a sailor and his wife – serious *aficionados* – came looking for me and a guitarist called Baldomero. He was a real *Gitano*, very funny, who groomed donkeys and dogs by day and tried to earn a living with his guitar by night.

The Engineer from the Monserrat

This sailor – an engineer on the Monserrat – whenever he arrived in Cádiz: Pericón and Baldomero;. Pericón and Baldomero, because his wife was crazy about us and loved the way I sang. Every trip was the same, until one day the

Monserrat came in and we were left waiting for the engineer. It was that way for seven or eight trips – the sailor never showed up looking for us. Of course, we were getting annoyed. This went on until one night when a berlin pulled up with all the curtains closed. The coachman got down, looking in La Havana until he saw me: "Pericón – come here, and bring Baldomero; I have a really good sailor."

It was him – the same sailor we'd sung for – the engineer from the Monserrat. We got into the coach, but he didn't say a word to us. He just told the coachman: "Go where I told you."

The coach went down through Puerta Tierra – it was a night with a *levante* – wind and rain – really scary! The coach kept going and going until we reached the cemetery gates. The coach stopped by the cemetery walls, and the sailor pulled open the curtains and shouted: "Dolores! I've brought you Pericón and Baldomero so you can hear them sing!"

I died! And Baldomero, he couldn't tell if he was playing the sixth string or the first. The poor guy had to play, though, and I had to sing. Every once in awhile, he'd put his head out and yell: "Dolores! Can you hear, sweetheart? Ay, I'm so sad you're not with me – you loved this so much!"

We were trembling. A whole hour there in the cemetery, singing, trembling, until he finally told the coachman: "Let's go."

We got in and left; he was crying and we were shaking.

"OK, where do you two want to be left off?"

Both of us at the same time: "Right here!"

The coach stopped before we got back to La Habana, he paid us - back then two *duros* each – and said: "Until next time."

And Baldomero, to me: "Yeah right!"

Of course, we never went again.

Come in, Baldomero

One night a wise guy undertaker came to the Aguaducho. He was called Nieto, and had his mortuary on Soperanis Street. He asked if Baldomero was there. When he found out he was, he went upstairs to a private room and told the waiter to tell Baldomero to come up in a half hour - that there was an *aficionado* who wanted to hear him play.

The undertaker went in the room with all the tools of his trade: a crucifix, a sheet, four candles ... He lay down on the table with everything assembled – like a real corpse – and waited for Baldomero ... Baldomero came up, the poor guy all excited that someone wanted to hear him play solo, and knocked. The undertaker said, in a hollow voice: "Come in, Baldomero. I've been waiting for you."

I don't know what went through that *Gitano*, but instead of getting scared, he grabbed the shears he used on donkeys and the corpse had to escape out the window; otherwise, Baldomero would have left it a real corpse.

For half your cemetery plot

It's that Baldomero was very superstitious and had a horrible fear of death.[61] So much that, if he even saw a funeral procession, he'd run away. But such is life, one day he fell ill.

Since Baldomero was sick, the guitarist Servando and me were in a *juerga* one night with a guy named Paco Benítez – a good *aficionado* who often hired us. During the *fiesta* I mentioned to him: "Don Francisco, do you know who's fallen ill?"

"Who, my son?"

---

[61] Fear and superstition about anything having to do with death is a cultural stereotype associated with *Gitanos*.

"Baldomero, the guitarist – poor guy, he's really bad."

"Man, that's too bad – that *Gitano* was such a good guy."

"Well, there you have it, he's in horrible shape."

Then Paco Benítez said:

"Look, I want to give you a little present to take to Baldomero for me; give it to him with a hug from me."

He gave us twenty *duros*; the next day Servando and me went to take it to him. We found his house on Corralón Street, asked one of his nieces for him, and went up to his room. The poor guy was sitting on a chair with two legs that looked like boots – all swollen. And with that body odor he had ... No more had we arrived than he started wailing: "Oh how happy I am to see you!"

"It's nothing, Baldomero – last night we were with Paco Benítez, and he sent you a present."

"Ay, my God! Thank you! I really appreciate it, because with what I have I can't even move."

And then Servando decided to say: "Don't you worry Baldomero. You're not going into the hole yet. Because we're your friends and we're here for you, and we'll raise enough for half your cemetery plot."

When he said that about the half cemetery plot, Baldomero had a look of horror come over him, that I've never seen again.

"Pericón! Did you hear what he just said? Half my cemetery plot?"

"Don't pay any attention. Don't pay attention; in three days you'll be out playing guitar again."

And him, crying: "I mean, he said I'm not going into the hole and that about the half cemetery plot?"

Anyway, we finally calmed him down and left. As soon as we were outside I said: "Man, Servando! What made you say that about the half cemetery plot? Can't you see the shape he's in and how he reacted?"

"I didn't mean any harm; I said it to calm him."

"Yeah, well you saw how calm he was!"

And he stayed so calm that in three days he died. Poor Baldomero – such a good guy, who groomed donkeys just as he played guitar.

For the love of a woman

There was a guy in Cádiz who presumed to be the most handsome and the best lover. He chatted up a woman in the barrio Santa María, jumping from one rooftop to the next to talk to her. One night, while jumping from one wall to another, he had the bad luck of falling down a well, where he drowned. Later, during Carnival, they made up a song about it:[62]

Por querer curiosear	Trying to be a busy body,
le sucedió	it happened
a un muchacho mu atrevío	to a daring young man
que en un pozo zambulló,	that he fell into a well.
lo tuvieron que sacar	They had to get him out
con un cordel.	with a line.
Tan sólo tuvo la culpa	All for
el amor de una mujer.	the love of a woman.
Nadando en el pozo	Swimming in the well
pasó su mal rato	that poor kid had a bad
aquel pobrecito	time.
y húmido, lánguido, pálido	And wet, languid, and pale,
me lo sacaron como un bonito,	they fished him out like a tuna.
todo el que estaba presente	All present
tomó el asunto	thought it

---

[62] This is sung as a *tanguillo* by Manolo Vargas, on D-14.

120

con mal jolgorio:	was hilarious:
tenías que ver la carita	you should have seen the face
que sacó Don Juan Tenorio.	that the Don Juan pulled.

1913

Since in Cádiz they make up songs about everything, when the year 1913 came – since it was a bad luck year – they came out with this one for Carnival:

A mil novecientos trece	Nineteen thirteen
buen se le puede llamar	should be called
el año de los balasos	the year of gunshots
o el de la calamidad,	or calamity.
el que no se daba un tiro	Whoever isn't shot
se colgaba por la nuez	is hung by the throat.
y el que no estaba chiflao	And whoever isn't flayed
daba coscorrones contra la pared.	is knocked against the wall.
Don Fermín, que tenía monomanía,	Don Fermín, who was obsessed,
se bebió dos botellas de lejía;	drank two bottles of lye.
y usté ve si perdimos la razón	You can see how we've lost all reason,
que hasta un señor caballero,	that even a gentleman
yo no sé aónde nació,	– I don't know where he's from –
a un muchacho basurero	wanted to ship a garbage boy
quiso facturarlo dentro de un cajón.	in a package.

This is because there was someone that year – a murderer or something – who caught a garbage boy and tried to mail him in a box, with his mouth taped and everything. He didn't succeed because an old woman called the police when she saw him go into a building with the garbage boy and come

121

out only with the box.

God took her ...

When I hung out in the Villa Rosa – the one in Ciudad Lineal, a gentleman stopped by – one who all the artists revered. He knew they did, and I don't know why, but he gravitated to those who paid the least attention to him. Of course, since I didn't know him, I didn't say anything to him; he went into a room alone and called the *Maître d'*: "Hey, who is the man near the entrance who didn't even say hello?"

"He's a singer from Cádiz; he's new."

"Well, ask him to come in here, and also call Manolo Badajoz."

So I went in with Manolo Badajoz, who told me:

"He's great – he pays very well."

But he didn't tell me that his wife had just died and that he'd been crazy about her.

We were in the room; the guy orders a bottle of whiskey and two dozen langoustines with mayonnaise. Wow! I was used to the *fiestas* in Cádiz – I went crazy, eating five or six *langoustines* and drinking two or three whiskies. Then I started singing: I sang *alegrías*, then *bulerías*, then *fandangos*. The guy didn't move – it seemed like he liked it, but he didn't move an inch. When we'd almost finished the bottle, I told Manolo Badajoz: "Manolo play malagueñas; I'm going to sing a *malagueña del Mellizo*."

Of course, I didn't know the guy's wife had died, and I decided to sing the malagueña that went "God took her".[63] I don't know why, but instead of saying "my mother", I said "my poor wife", after saying "why did God take her?". The man

---

[63] This *malagueña* was recorded, with a somewhat different verse, by Manolo Caracol on his anthology (D-4). Pericón provides Mellizo's original verse in Part 5, "Enrique el Mellizo".

got up, crying, and came towards me; when I'd finished singing, he came over and slapped me across the face. Crying, but what a slap – then he hugged me, still crying, and said: "I'm sorry! I'm sorry!"

"Man! Do you know what you just did? You slapped me silly!"

"I'm sorry, I'm sorry! I'm just emotional – please – repeat that verse – sing it again for me!"

"Of course, my pleasure, but wait a minute while I get upon this ledge"

And Manolo Badajoz almost broke his guitar laughing: *"Ole, viva Cai!"*

4. ANIMALS ARE REALLY SOMETHING!

Cadiz: Youth attacked by a "vampire"

CÁDIZ, 11. (Cifra). - Upon leaving a movie theater, where a vampire movie was shown, José González Valle, 18, commented to his companions: "These things can be true, because a vampire can appear and attack you at any time."

A passerby heard this, who, by coincidence, had a marked deformity of the teeth, involving larger than normal incisors. The individual in question thought the youth's remark was directed at him, and, without a word, attacked him hitting him first on the head and then biting him.

José González, who thought that it was a real vampire that attacked him, told his story immediately at the nearest police station. The aggressor turned out to be a man known by the nickname "The Wolf", from Gitanilla del Carmelo Street, of this capital. He explained to the police inspector that he attacked the youth because he thought the talk of vampires alluded to him.

NEWS ITEM APPEARING IN THE DAILY *INFORMACIONES*, MADRID, JULY 11, 1974

Ole, viva Cádiz!

Open wide, son

When I was a kid, I was always starving. Since no matter how much I ate, I was still hungry, I went to the meat stand my mother had next to the Tres Reyes. There, without her noticing, I stuffed myself on pieces of raw meat.

From the raw meat I got a tapeworm; they called the doctor: "Listen, this kid won't stop eating, he finishes eating and is starving again in two minutes."

"All right Ma'am, tomorrow morning give him a piece of codfish and then nothing else; I'll come by in the afternoon to see what I think."

So she did; she gave me the codfish, and the doctor came in the afternoon: "Doctor, he's been crying all day, but I didn't give him anything else."

"Very good, very good. Bring me a basin full of milk."

My mother found a basin, filled it with two liters of milk, and the doctor: "Open wide, son."

When I opened my mouth, and since the *bicho* was starving and dying of thirst, it stuck its head out of my mouth, and went for the milk. The doctor grabbed it, and started pulling and pulling. He kept on pulling for two hours. Never in my life have I seen such a long one! They rolled it into a big ball; my brother calculated it was at lease forty meters ...

Of course, after that I didn't eat as much as before – it was that *bicho* that was eating everything and leaving me starving.

The singing and dancing turkey

When I sang in Puerto Real with Perico Pavón, I remember one night when they presented a guy with a number where his turkey sang and danced.

The guy didn't get paid anything – instead they let him raffle a bottle of *aguardiente* or cognac, which the owner gave him – that was his pay. First he sold tickets – he auctioned them off, getting a *perra gorda* for one, a *perra chica* for another, until he sold them all and had the raffle.

Then came the singing and dancing turkey. He had a cage under the stage, on top of a hot plate. When he brought it out, the floor of the cage was red hot – he announced: "Dear public, dear public! Now you'll see something you've never seen in your life: A turkey that sings and dances! It's incredible!"

"And you, turkey!", he continued, "I want you to show

this respectable public your talent. Show them the dances and songs you perform inside your cage!"

No sooner had he put the turkey in the cage than the poor turkey started jumping up and down, squawking, the way they do. Because, of course, every time its feet touched the floor they were fried, poor thing.

That went on for about two weeks. Of course, everyday he'd have to buy a new turkey, because by the end of the show the poor thing was dead – fried. The guy took it out and ate it – everyday, after the show, he had his singing and dancing turkey for dinner – what a guy!

Oh, how funny!

There were a few *Gitanos* in the Barrio Santa María who opened a place called Cante Jondo – it was on the road near Puerta Tierra. Whenever a coach with a *juerga* went by, they'd come out and yell: "*Cante jondo, cante jondo!*"

As if to say "Come in here and see something you've never seen anywhere in Spain." Well, regarding the Cante Jondo, I remember a woman from Sevilla – a jewelry merchant – wealthy, fortyish, and head over heels in love with me and my twenty-something years ... This woman loved funny things, and because of that, that's all she ever wanted ... finding funny stuff; there was no changing her. Once, when she came to Cádiz, she said: "Pericón, I want you to find me something really funny."

"All right, let's go to Cante Jondo, and you'll see."

So, I went to Cante Jondo and talked to one of the owners: "Look, there is this woman from Sevilla who wants to see dancing and listen to *cante*, but it should all be funny – really funny, you know? And then prepare four or five rabbits in rice."

The next time I saw Carmen – her name was Carmen –

I told her: "It's all arranged, Carmen, this Saturday they'll put on the funny show."

Carmen and I showed up at the Cante Jondo that Saturday at ten thirty. As we entered, there was wine everywhere – the cabinets full of bottles of white wine and two big barrels, also full. We went into a room and told the owner to get the artists.

You should have seen the artists: seven or eight *Gitanos* from the *barrio*, one danced and the other sang. The *fiesta* got underway... Carmen loved it, dancing, singing, drinking ... Finally, I said: "It's time for the rabbits with rice."

I clapped my hands, the owner came in with a platter, put it on the table. I was ready to dig in, when the owner said: "I hope you enjoy the rabbits."

"All right, let's see – I'm starving."

No more had I said this when the son of a bitch opened the pot, and out jumped two cats. They were alive and crazy from being cooped up. You could practically see Carmen's wisdom teeth from how she was laughing.

"Oh, Pericón, that's so funny!"

"How's that funny, Carmen? I don't think it's funny."

She laughed and laughed, but I didn't laugh at all, because I was starving and all I wanted was to eat.

Real funny.

The spirit of a fireman

Poor Capinetti. As great a guitarist as he was, he was hopeless once he put his guitar down. I remember once when he was always going on about this cat of his: "Listen, Pericón, I'm really worried about my cat."

"What's wrong with it, José?"

"Well, it's just that every time I throw a match on the floor, the cat comes running to put it out."

"Boy, that's a strange cat you have, José."

"I'm telling you."

Then I had an idea: "Listen José, they say Ignacio Espeleta is a spiritualist. Maybe he can tell you what's up with your cat."

So, a few days later, we were at the Turisbar, when Capinetti shows up; I said to Ignacio: "Hey Ignacio, let's see if you can explain what's going on. Capinetti has a very strange cat."

And Capinetti: "Yeah, Ignacio, I'll tell you, because Pericón told me you're a spiritualist."

Of course, he wasn't a spiritualist at all – it was all a big joke.

"Yes, son, I'm a spiritualist. What's wrong with your cat?"

"Well, it turns out that every time I throw a match on the floor, the cat comes running and puts it out."

"All right Capinetti – don't say any more. You know what that is? It's the spirit of a fireman trapped in a cat's body."

There it is – I got it!

Once we happened to be talking about sicknesses with Ignacio Espeleta and there was a guy who kept complaining about his stomach aches, this, that, and the other, until Ignacio said:

"Maybe you have the same thing I once had; I was over twenty years raging about my stomach, until a village doctor figured it out. I'd gone to this little town with some friends to buy livestock. We got to the casino: one drink, and then another, but the doctor noticed I wasn't drinking and asked: 'What's wrong? Why aren't you drinking?'

'It's that I have this stomach problem.'

'Well come by my office in the morning, and we'll see

if we can figure it out.'

Since I'd already been to a hundred doctors, I thought I'd maybe go just to see which new illness he'd find. So I went the next day, he looked in my eyes and said: 'Take down your pants and underpants, and lie down with your ass in the air.'

Since he was a doctor, I did what he said, but wondered what he was up to. I felt him putting Vaseline in my ass – I started to worry – then I felt something metal going in, when he suddenly said: 'There it is – I got it!'

He started pulling and pulling, until he pulled out a rat that had been living in my stomach; a huge rat that had gotten in when it was little without me noticing, and then grew there. Since then, I've been a new man."

The goat from Medina

I remember a guy from Medina who loved me a lot. Every time he came to Cádiz – every week – he called me to sing for him. He loved it and I loved it too because he paid well and treated me very well. Once we were in a *fiesta* and he said: "Pericón, I want to take you to Medina."

"No, don José, don't worry about it."

"What do you mean 'no' – don't be silly. You come with me to Medina and I'll give you a nice present. Also, look, my daughter is sick at home and I'd like you to sing her two or three *fandangos*. I talk a lot about you at home, and my daughter keeps saying she wants to meet you."

"All right, sure, I'll go with you."

So I went with him to Medina to a farmhouse he had – with beautiful lands around it. We got to the farmhouse. The poor little girl was sick in bed, so I sang her eight or ten *fandangos*, did some slight of hand tricks ... In all, I was there until about three in the morning, and by that time I was really drunk. Don José said: "Well, I'll get the car to take you home."

"Sure, but do you think you could give me a few chickens or hens to take home?"

"Shit, man, I'm sorry! The thing is that I don't have any chickens around here – they are in the other part of the farm – too far to walk at this hour, in our condition. But I can give you a goat."

When he told me about the goat, I got really excited – I was crazy! Since I was going to Cádiz alone in the car, he tied up the goat for me, and I got home alone with the goat. I went up to my room with the goat, went in, tied the goat to the bedpost, and put the envelope with my money on the night table. A green envelope with four thousand *pesetas* – four thousand *pesetas* in those days! I went to bed and slept. After a while, my wife came from her errands: "But what's this that you brought home?"

"A goat, can't you see? A goat that they gave me."

"And they didn't give you any money?"

"Of course – it's in the green envelope – four thousand pesetas."

"Green envelope? What green envelope?"

"Girl, it's on the night table."

"On the night table? There's no envelope on the night table."

"Shit – are you saying there's no green envelope?"

I jumped out of bed, and sure enough, no envelope – the damn goat had eaten it; the damn goat! Of course – goats eat paper and had seen the green envelope and ate it along with the four thousand *pesetas*. I didn't hear a thing – I nearly died!

We took the goat and sold it – we sold it to a butcher called el Chino.

Damn goat!

The hunchback parrot

One year during Carnival some guys got the idea of putting a hunchback in a cage and raffling him off, like he was a parrot. They got the hunchback and put him in a big cage they'd made and then went all over Cádiz selling raffle tickets for the parrot. They'd get to a bar carrying the parrot on a litter and went through the crowd selling tickets, and getting wine for the parrot. You should have seen the hunchback parrot's tongue hanging out asking for wine. Between one and another, for fun, people gave the parrot glasses of wine until the poor thing was wasted. It was like that all day, from place to place with the tickets, until nighttime when they got together to split up the proceeds.

But by the third day of Carnival there was no parrot or hunchback – nothing. I ran into one of the guys and asked:

"What's up? Did you raffle the parrot?"

"Yeah, we raffled him all right – the police won."

Because one of the times he was asking for wine, already drunk, the hunchback parrot let his tongue go too far they carted him off to the police station – that way the police ended up winning the raffle of the hunchback parrot – poor thing.

The chimpanzee butler

One night in La Habana, a *señor* showed up with a girl from one of the brothels asking for a singer and guitarist to go to a *fiesta*. Baldomero happened to be there, so he called me and we started the *juerga*.

"Where do you think we should go?" the guy asked, attentively.

131

"Well, we could go to Vito – its quiet there, or if you like, we could go to a room here, have a *media botella*, listen a little, and then go to the restaurant."

So we went to a room, and sang for awhile – the guy was very generous and attentive. He gave the waiter a tip worth more than the bottle. I said to myself "This is a real catch!" From the room we went to the Vito restaurant. As soon as we arrived I told the waiter about the jewel we'd brought. We went into a reserved room – more wine, more ham, more *cante*, ... And he gave the girl any little thing she wanted – a box of candy for her sister, another box for another sister ... Between one thing and another, the guy ran out of money. When it came time to pay us he said: "*Señores*, you'll have to forgive me, but I can't pay you now. But if you don't mind, I'll pay you tomorrow at my hotel."

And then he went off with the girl. We went to sleep, and the next day me and Baldomero met at La Habana to go to the hotel to collect. We got to the hotel, showed the concierge the calling card he'd given us, and he told us to go up to room 106 – where the gentleman was staying.

We got to the door, and I was trying to convince Baldomero that he should knock, since he was older. He knocked, and in a while we heard footsteps and the door opened. But instead of the guy, it was a chimpanzee! A chimpanzee that the guy had trained to be a butler! Of course, as soon as we saw that *bicho,* we jumped up and raced down the stairs, taking them four at a time. Poor Baldomero, running the best he could, and the concierge peeing his pants laughing at the chimpanzee joke.

When everyone calmed down, the concierge called the gentleman and he came down and paid us himself.

I was the octopus' pimp

There was a time when I used to go fishing for shellfish – I fished and fished, and one day, I caught an octopus – you should've seen it... Then I remembered something I'd heard about octopi – if they see something pretty, they hold it in their tentacles. They go walking along the sea floor, and if they see a colored stone or any other pretty thing, they hold it in their tentacles and when the tide goes out, they go to their cave and hide whatever they have.

So, instead of killing it, I let it go again in the water and took notice of where it had its cave. Every afternoon, when the tide went out, I went to the Caleta and waited for it to go out until I could reach the octopus' cave. When I got to the entrance, there were always two or three rings, a bracelet, ... I took whatever there was, without telling anyone, and then sold them to a guy called Manolo el Pajarero, who had a stand in the market, and who sold jewelry and stuff like that. I'd go by and say: "Let's see, Manuel, what do you think of this?"

He'd look at what I had – of course some of it was junk, but other times there were real gold rings and earrings.

"Well look, these earrings are gold and so is this ring, but this one is worthless. So, Pericón, I can give you thirty-eight *pesetas*."

Of course, during that time, I took the thirty-eight *pesetas*, I felt like the richest man on earth. The next day I waited for the tide to come in and go out to see what the octopus had left me in the cave. And sure enough – more rings, bracelets, and earrings that the octopus had caught in its tentacles. I had all of Cádiz crazy – everyone was saying, "where is he getting all that money?"

Because in a *fiesta*, they gave you a *duro*, and there wasn't a *fiesta* every day. So, how could this Pericón go around everyday buying drinks for his friends, and buying suits he didn't even need?

That's how I had all of Cádiz crazy, until one day a fisherman called Mangoli put his hook in my octopus' cave and fished it out. He left me devastated – completely devastated! It's that I was the octopus' pimp and no one knew that I was being kept by an octopus; I'd been with it for at least three years, until this Mangoli killed it and cut my head off. Whenever I'd see Mangoli around the barrio de la Viña, I'd say to him: "Mangoli, you ruined me! Ruined me!"

The bicho on the beach

Back when we were trying to earn a living at night in Cádiz, we'd first do a pass by the places that were open to see how things were – Tres Reyes, the Petí Kursal, ... If we saw people in a *juerga*, we got the picture: so-and-so, after a few more drinks, would be at the *venta* Casablanca. So we would head out to Casablanca, where there were also artists, *cupleistas*, and so on.

The *fiestas* at Casablanca happened later, after 3:30, when the cabarets in Cádiz let out. While the people arrived, the ten or twelve of us artists sat and waited.

I remember one night in August with one of those full moons; we were looking at how beautiful the beach was.

I got up and took a walk on the terrace to see the moon and beach better. No sooner had I gone out, than I saw in the sand this weird *bicho* making horrible sounds and dragging itself along.

I jumped up and ran inside to the others; when they saw the *bicho*, how it moved and screeched, we all ran away, horrified, from that monster.

Until finally, a waiter came and explained that it wasn't

really a *bicho* at all. It was Magaña, who was out there that night.   He had attached a braid of garlic to his butt for a tail, and put a champagne ice bucket on his head, which reflected the moonlight – and then those screeches – it was scary.

This Magaña was always pulling off jokes like this. He'd start off sitting with us, looking for work, but then he'd get a devilish idea in his head... Without thinking twice, he'd disappear – we wouldn't see him until he showed up with one of his tricks.

Pericón, thief!

Back when there was no work in Cádiz, around two or three in the morning, we all would go out to a *venta* called Vito's Restaurant, out beyond Puerta Tierra.   By Puerta Tierra, there was always a dog waiting for us – a dog that was practically human-like.   It was me and Antonio el Herrero; as soon as the dog saw us, he'd follow us to Vito's Restaurant.

The place usually had five or six tables with *señoritos* waiting for the singers to arrive.   So, when we got there, one or the other would call me over.   I'd go sit with the *señorito* and started in telling him, or the girl he'd brought: "Look at this dog and how smart he is."

"What does he do?"

"You'll see – Smokey!"

And Smokey came over – he was a kind of wolf dog.

"Put a ten *céntimos* coin on his nose."

Smokey stood still, and I clapped my hands: "One, two, three!"

The dog caught the coin – he tossed it with his nose and caught it in his mouth.   Then he ran outside to the hiding place he had among the trees, hid the coin, and came back for more. In this way, the dog spent the night getting *perras gordas* and *perras chicas* ...

The next morning, when the store next door opened, the dog went to his treasure site, took out four or five coins, and went to the store. He threw them on the counter, and the owner knew to give him four or five rolls. He ate the rolls and if he wanted more, he'd go back to his hole for more coins and back to the store for more rolls.

This went on day after day ...

One night I was completely tapped out and *canino* – two or three days without earning a *peseta*. I started in thinking about the dog – where was he hiding his money?

I watched him get a coin and run off, so I followed, without him noticing, hiding myself among the trees. I watched him stop, start digging, hide the coin, and head back to the restaurant. I moved in and dug – shit! Over eighteen *pesetas*! I filled my pockets and ran back to the restaurant before the dog returned. I went in and sat next to the guitarist, as if nothing had happened.

But a minute later, the dog came in from his trip outside – you should've seen his face – he'd realized what'd happened, so he started in sniffing everyone. First the pianist – sniff, sniff. Then the cook – sniff. Then a *señorito* – sniff, sniff...

I was dying, watching all of this; then he came up to me – I'm trembling and pale. He started sniffing and sniffing, with me pretending nothing was happening, turning my face away, until that dog got up on his hind legs and said, in a dog's voice: "PERICÓN, THIEF!"

I jumped out of my chair and took off running – all the coins spilling out on the floor... I'd never seen anything like it – he was just like a person!

Of course, this is the kind of story you tell, and no one believes you.

Ay! My children!

Near my house in Cádiz lived a woman with a beautiful cat. When I went out on my balcony the cat meowed until I gave it something to eat. Since I gave it fish bones and stuff like that, the cat loved me.

But one day she gave birth to six or seven little kittens, and when I went out on the balcony, she was in the middle of the street waiting for food, when a truck came by and ran her over.

The poor little animal, bleeding all over, dragged itself to the door of her house to die with her children. But her owner wouldn't let her in, because she'd stain the house with her blood. The cat insisted and insisted, and her owner hit her with the broom, so she'd finish dying in the street.

The poor thing, once she saw she couldn't die next to her kittens started to cry desperately, and, in her last sob said:

"Ay! My children!"

I saw this from my balcony, horrified, when I heard her say that in her cat's voice, I started to shake and had such an attack of nerves that I had to go inside.

Goodbye, hunchbacked asshole!

On Palma Street, in Cádiz, there was a hunchback who had a coal store. In the coal store, he kept a parrot – what a parrot! It had heard a recording of Canalejas:

Ay, Rocio,	Ay, Rocio,
manojo de claveles,	bunch of carnations,
capullito florecío,	flowered bonnet,
por pensar en tu querer	thinking of your love,
yo voy a perder el sentío.	I'm losing my mind.

137

The parrot sang this just like on the record. Of course, anyone who passed by was drooling over the parrot.

One day a *señorito* happened by, and seeing all the people listening to the parrot, stopped to listen himself. He was so impressed that he went to the hunchback and said: "Listen, is your parrot for sale?"

But the coal seller wouldn't sell the parrot for anything; he could have given him anything at all, and he still wouldn't sell.

"I'll give you whatever you ask."

"No, no – I'm not selling this parrot."

He insisted a few more times, but the hunchback kept saying "no" – no, he wouldn't sell the parrot for anything in the world. When the *señorito* saw it was no use he said: "Well, look, I'll leave my card in case you change your mind and decide to sell – remember, I'll pay anything you ask."

The hunchback took the card and put it away.

One day, feeding the parrot a potato, the hunchback put his finger in the cage; the parrot bit it so hard it broke the finger. You should have seen the hunchback – he grabbed the parrot and gave it such a beating.

"You son of the Great Whore parrot! I shit on your mother!"

He hit it again and again...

The next day the parrot was mute, then the next – not a sound, completely mute, and the hunchback: "What's wrong son, what's wrong?"

He took it out and put it in the sun so it would sing, but it didn't sing. It was like that day after day. Of course, the hunchback thought to himself: "This son of a bitch is mute, it won't sing or talk, anymore. I'm going to call that *señorito*, and sell it to him."

So he got out the card and called the number.

"Hello, is this don Enrique?"

"Yes – what is it?"

"Listen, I'm the hunchback from the coal store – you wanted to buy my parrot?"

"Of course! What's up?"

"Well, you see, I have some bills I need to pay, and was thinking of selling my parrot, so I thought of you."

"*Hombre*! Wonderful! I'll be there in a little bit."

Sure enough, the señorito was there in a half hour. The parrot was watching all of this and listening. The hunchback said to the *señorito*: "You can see what happened, so I thought of you."

"No problem, I really appreciate it; here are the fifteen thousand *pesetas* you asked for: one, two, three, four ... fifteen thousand *peseta* bills."

The hunchback picked up the cage: "Here you are; I'm so sad to part with it."

As soon as the *señorito* took the cage and the parrot saw that it no longer belonged to the hunchback, it turned and said: "GOODBYE, HUNCHBACKED ASSHOLE! NOW YOU CAN'T HIT ME ANYMORE!"

The hunchback, on hearing the parrot say that, wished he had asked the *señorito* for two thousand *duros* more.

Animals are really something!

The aficionado cat

In the world of flamenco there have been so many nutty things that one has to go along with, without saying anything. I've experienced so much, but then when I tell people, no one believes me.

There was a man in Cádiz who often called me to sing; he liked my singing and would go all night and into the morning. Around eight in the morning, when I said I had to go, he'd say: "No, Pericón, a little longer. Come to my house with me to sing a few *fandangos* to my cat."

If I didn't go, he wouldn't pay me, so when time came to collect, I had no choice but to finish the *juerga* with his cat. We'd go to his house, and when we got there, his wife, who knew about his quirk, got the cat and put it up on a table. The animal was terrified up there, with me singing it two or three *fandangos* so the guy could be happy seeing his cat listening to *cante*.

After doing this two or three times, I figured out the *aficionado* cat trick; when I saw it was getting light, I started asking to go to his house: "Look, right now I'm in great form to sing to your cat."

That way, we'd go, I'd sing to the cat, he'd pay me, and I could go home and go to bed.

A war story

There's a guy in Cádiz, still alive, who's a good friend of mine, and even a bigger liar than me. We'd get together to talk and he'd tell me stories. One day he told me about when he was in the war.

"Pericón, I'm going to tell you about something that happened to me during the war: we were about to take a town, when, when I don't know what happened, but the captain said: 'Save yourselves!'

So of course we were all running all over the place – some in one direction, others in another, and I ended up going cross-country. But Pericón! A day and a night, another day and night – I thought I'd starve to death, until I got an idea. I took out my sword and stuck it in the ground. And what do you know? I got a potato! My God, when I heard the ground make a 'craaack' sound, I pulled it out and found the potato – as hungry as I was!

But look, no sooner had I had the potato than a dog came running up – one of those wolf dogs, also starving, the poor thing. Of course, when it saw I had a potato, it came after me – you should have seen it! I was shaking, thinking it would eat me and the potato. I don't know what I did, but I stuck the sword back in the ground in front of me and closed my eyes, with the dog already upon me ...

And was that dog coming after me hard! It didn't see the sword, because when I opened my eyes, the sword was still there with a half a dog on either side of it.

The dog came with such violence that even its tail was cut in two, with half a tail on one side and the other half on the other."

That's what my friend Joselito de la Rita told me.

The amphibious bicho

When I hung out in the Tres Reyes, there was a captain of a ferry boat from Cádiz to Tangier, a very good aficionado. We called him don José of the Capitana, because whenever he was in Cádiz he'd get a girl from the Capitana brothel.

One day this don José of the Capitana came by Tres Reyes with a jackal dog – one of those wolf dogs. He tied it up to one of the columns – what a dog with a silver tail and those eyes. He called me to sing with the guitarist Servando. I said to him: "Don José, what a beautiful animal."

"Yeah, it's a jackal, a wolf."

"A real wolf?"

"A real wolf! Jackal. If you like, I'll give him to you."

"No, *hombre*, don José, thanks very much, but ..."

"What do you mean no? *Hombre*, I'll give him to you. I go to Tangier tomorrow and I'll get another one."

So then I remembered that I had promised to sell a wolf

dog to a guy with a *bodega* in the Plaza Candelaria. This store that had jugs of *valdapeñas*, like you've never seen. When I remembered, I thought to myself "I'll sell this to Pepín" (the owner of the *bodega*).

Sure enough, when the *juerga* was over, I acted like I wanted the dog, and he gave it to me.

I then lived on Ustariz Street. I went with the dog to Ustariz, got to my house, tied it up in the kitchen, and closed the doors. When I got up the next morning, the dog had eaten two mops and a broom. The dog had some scary fangs!

So I said to myself "OK, I'm taking this dog to Pepín," because Pepín wanted a dog to guard his *bodega* in the Plaza Candelaria."

I got to his house – he lived on Sagasta Street – and went upstairs with the *bicho*. It didn't want to go up – I had to drag it to Pepín's house. I knocked and the maid answered.

"Who is it?"

"Excuse me, is don José in – Pepín?"

"Yes, but he's sleeping."

"Could you tell him that Pericón was here with the wolf dog?"

Then I heard Pepín's voice: "Pericón, come in."

I went in with the dog – that jackal dog – the *bicho* was flopped on the floor while Pepín looked down from the bed, and asked: "What is that? Is that a wolf dog, Pericón?"

"It's a wolf dog – I wouldn't lie to you. Can't you see it's a jackal?"

"Is it tame?"

"Tame? See for yourself!"

And I put my face next to its face so it could have torn my throat out if it wanted to, and I even gave it a kiss.

"Ah yes, it seems tame! How much do you want for it?"

"Well, Pepín, the jackal dog belongs to a woman, and

she wants 500 *pesetas* for it, and if you wanted to give me a present on top of it ..."

He got his wallet and gave me 600 *pesetas* – 100 *duros* for the woman and 20 *duros* for me, and said: "Take it to my *bodega* and tell Romerito, the guy in charge, to tie it up, and then let it loose inside at night when he closes in case someone tries to rob the place."

Later that night, around 2:30 or 3:00, Romerito was at my house:"Pericón!"

"Who is it?"

"Me, Romerito! Come on, get dressed and come with me."

I thought it was a *juerga* with Pepín, that he wanted me to sing. I got dressed, and when I came out to the street, Romerito: "Ruination! You've ruined the *señorito!*"

"What happened?"

"What happened? Do you know what that *bicho* did in the *bodega*? It ate the four taps off the wine jugs and is swimming in *valdepeñas*. There's a huge river of *valdepeñas* running out on the street."

When I got to the *bodega*, Pepín: "You've ruined me! What kind of a *bicho* did you sell me?"

I didn't dare say anything, but: "*Hombre*, don José, a wolf dog, a jackal."

"That's no wolf dog! It ate the four taps ... Get it out of here right now – I don't want to see it again, or I'll kill it!"

So I took it the next day. Since I wanted to get rid of it, I gave it to my brother Ricardo, and he went and sold it to a captain who saw it on Ancha street and liked its profile. The captain called my brother and asked: "Excuse me, could you tell me if that *bicho* is tame?"

"Of course, can't you see it is a jackal?"

"Would you sell it?"

"Yes sir, for thirty *duros*."

"Fine – it's a deal."

He gave him the thirty *duros* and sent him with a card to the barracks that were in the park. My brother went and left the dog, as instructed.

But three or four days later, the *bicho* escaped and hid under the waterfall, the waterfall in the park. It came out at night and every night it ate three or four ducks. They found the ducks' skins because it grabbed them by the necks, dug in its claws, opened them up like prickly pears, and ate the meat. Of course, everyone was upset about the duck skins. Until one night: the park guards tracked it, and as it went for some ducks, they shot and killed it.

It made such a scandal in Cádiz that they later came out with some verses during Carnival – verses about it eating three or four ducks.

That's when I realized how dangerous these *bichos* can be. When a lion or a tiger, or some other nasty *bicho* goes after them trying to eat them, they put their tail between their legs and pee on it. Since their pee is so strong and acidic, if the lion or tiger gets too close they'll hit the nasty *bicho* on the nose with their tail. When that urine gets into its eyes, it's left senseless, anesthetized, and that way they can get away.

Avita

Finally, we had at home a little dog named Ava. I named it that because of my friendship with Ava Gardner, who loved me a lot, and I remember her by naming our dog after her. It's registered with that name. It is a little animal with such an amazing intelligence that it seems human. When we lived on Caramuel Street, the first thing it did every morning was go to the window to watch people go by...

Once our son Jumán kept bugging us to go to Cádiz for the summer. So, we finally went. We left the dog with our other son, Antonio. A week later we received a letter saying that the poor dog was miserable – it wouldn't eat or drink, it wouldn't eat a thing, and, of course, the poor thing was starving – the dog looked like a skeleton.

When it was time to come home, we arrived at the Atocha Station, took a taxi, and when we got close to the house, the dog – who didn't even look like herself – was in the window looking around everywhere, until she saw us and started crying like a real person. When we opened the door and went in, she was there with a handkerchief crying, just like a regular person. Of course, my wife, who knew a lot about the dog because she took care of it, said that poor Avita thought we had died when we went to Cádiz.

5. REMEMBERING THE MASTERS

*I*n Cádiz there were lots of great artists, but the ones I paid the most attention to were the Mellizos – the sons of Enrique el Mellizo: Antonio el Mellizo and Enrique el Morcilla; also Aurelio.

Enrique el Mellizo

Manuel Ortega, Caracol el del Bulto, told me a lot about Enrique el Mellizo. We'd sit and have coffee, while I kept asking him about Enrique – he'd tell me about him: "Listen, Pericón, when I was a little kid, Enrique really liked me – he often said: 'Manolito, come along with me.' We'd go down along the Campo del Sur to Capuchinos to sing for the crazies. Other times, he'd go to the sea wall and sing to the sea ... When he got drunk, he'd become so inspired that in the middle of the night, all by himself, he would go down to Capuchinos to sing for the crazies; other times by the sea wall to sing things that made even a bald man's hair stand on end:

Me asomé a la muralla	I went to the sea wall
y me respondió el viento:	and the wind replied:
¿a qué vienen tantos suspiros	Why cry so much
si ya no hay remedio?	when it's no use?

When he got like that, you could offer him all the money in the world, and he wouldn't sing for you. He'd rather go off alone to sing for the poor crazies or to the sea ..."

Furthermore, as the father of Caracol told me, he didn't live from his *cante* – and singing like he did. Instead, he worked as a *matarife* in the slaughterhouse. Everything he sang and everything he knew was because of his love for the *cante*. When he finished his work at the slaughterhouse, before going home – and he lived next to it – he'd go into the church of Santa María to hear the priests sing. Then he'd go home with his bag of fried fish, humming the music he'd heard, putting it into a flamenco form, without knowing any music – without being a musician or anything. The things he did made you say "but how is this possible?"

Because his double *malagueña* came from there – from Gregorian Chant; since it didn't have a *salida* – he invented the *Perdón*:[64]

Perdón, Dios mío;	God, pardon me;
perdón y clemencia;	pardon and clemency,
perdón y indulgencia;	pardon and indulgence,
perdón y piedad.	pardon and piety.

Then he'd come out with the *malagueña*:

Se la llevó Dios	God took her,
a la pobre mare mía	my poor mother.
¿Por qué se la llevó Dios?	Why did God take her?
si era que Él la quería,	If it was that He wanted her,
eso lo respeto yo.	I can understand that,
Pero s'ha llevao toa mi alegría.	but he took away my only joy.

And that without knowing how to read or write – just with the great sense of music that *Gitano* had.

One year, around Christmas, the priest from Santa María, who'd heard about Enrique's love of his music, called

---

[64] Pericón sings this on D-7.

him and asked him to sing some Christmas carols on Christmas Eve. What a commotion in Santa María when people found out that Enrique and his three children were going to sing Christmas carols. The place filled up with a frightening number of *Gitanos*. The Mass began – first the priest came out singing, answered by a chorus of the Mellizos. The old people in the corners started – very softly – "*Ole, ole, ole, Manuela, arsa Manuela.*" Then again the priest, and again the chorus, and again the old people – this time louder – "*Ole arsa Manuela*". And then again the priest and the chorus, until the old people couldn't take it anymore, and right inside the church: "¡*Ole, ole, ole!*" They raised the roof, because they just couldn't stand or resist the duende of the Mellizos.

There were stories like these without end. A new governor came to Cádiz – you should have seen him – he made everything close by three in the morning. When two or three people were on the street, a *sereno* came to disperse them, because it was past midnight. Well, one night Enrique had tied one on and went down to sing to the sea, right in front of the governor's mansion. A *sereno* came and said: "Hey you! don't you know you can't sing at this hour?"

But once he arrested him, the governor came out on his balcony: "Hey *sereno*! Do me a favor and let him keep singing."

How that man must have sung! And of course, the guard left, and Mellizo, on his bender, kept singing.

Something like this also happened in Sevilla with Manuel Torre. Enrique was with Manuel Torre one day, when Torre invited him for a drink of *aguardiente* in a bar on Sierpes Street – a bar that only had *aguardiente*. It also didn't allow singing – there was a sign saying "Singing Prohibited". None of the Sevilla artists could sing there. But that day Enrique got the urge and started singing *Montañés* songs like no one else could. Of course, the *Montañés* owner, instead of telling him

148

to be quiet or to leave, kept inviting him to drinks so he'd keep singing – he drank thirty-six glasses of *aguardiente* without it costing him a *real* and with *cante* prohibited.

Another time – also in Sevilla – his son Antonio told me (of the sons, he was the one who talked the most about his father) that some men had hired him and he was singing in El Duque in a room. In the room next door was Antonio Chacón, also in a *fiesta*. You can imagine how this man must have sung, because, no sooner had he begun his salida to the *malagueña,* when Chacón heard and said: "*Señores* – silence please!"

Chacón got down on his knees and crawled to the next room where Enrique was singing. He put his hands on Enrique's knees and waited until he finished singing. When he was done, he got up, kissed him and said "You're the greatest on Earth!"

Any true artist who heard him thought the same.

When Manuel Torre was doing his military service in Cádiz, Enrique was in a party with his friends in a place called La Primera de Cádiz; it had a balcony onto Canalejas Street. When Manuel found out Enrique was there, he was so crazy about hearing him sing, he waited for someone to come out of the room, to get him to invite him into the *fiesta.* He went in, stood in the corner near the balcony, Enrique started singing. That *cante* of his impressed Torre so much that if he hadn't caught himself in time, he would have fallen off of the balcony. With the things that Mellizo did in his *cante*!

Enrique el Mellizo.

Antonio el Mellizo

I liked the way Antonio el Mellizo sang *malagueña* more than his brother Enrique. It's that Antonio, with such a melodic voice, gave it such a tremendous feeling – particularly the *malagueña chica* – that this guy would make you cry, with his little voice that was all heart – as if it were a knife ...

He also had the ability to get the most out of all the verses – making them greater. You'd hear him sing them and they sounded like new verses. I remember one *malagueña* verse he sang that still gives me goose bumps:

Por su alma,	For her soul,
toítas las noches le rezo	every night I pray
a mi mare por su alma,	to my mother for her soul;
cojo el retrato y lo beso	I take her picture and I kiss it,
y entra en mi alma una calma	and a calm comes over my soul,
porque sólo en mi mare pienso	because I think only of my mother.

And he'd finish:

¿Dónde la enterraron?	If I only knew the place
Si yo subiera el sitio	where they buried my mother,
aonde a mi mare enterraron,	Where did they bury her?
yo sacaría los huesos de mi mare	I'd take my mother's bones
pa en mi casa embalsamarlos	to embalm them in my house
y toas las noches rezarle.	and pray to her every night.

Of course, then you couldn't help but cry...

Then there were the things that occurred to him. Lots of times, in a *fiesta*, when the bill came, the *señoritos* would fight over it – everyone wanting to be the one who paid. The waiter would bring the bill: "No – don't let so-and-so pay."

"This time I'm paying."

"No – no way – I'm paying."

Of course, during these arguments there was always someone who got away without paying anything. Because of this, once Antonio el Mellizo came over and said to me: "Listen, Pericón, next time we're in a *fiesta*, and there's a *señorito* who doesn't get to pay, let's do the Bitter Fountain trick. You look to see if there is someone who wanted to pay, but didn't get to. Go up to him and tell him that I'm sick, with a very bad rheumatism, and I need to go to the baths at the Bitter Fountain Spa, but of course, I don't have the money ..."

Exactly as planned, I went up to a *señorito* and said: "How did you like Antonio el Mellizo?"

"*Hombre*! What an old-school singer! He was marvelous!"

All the time, Antonio was playing the part of someone with rheumatism, sitting on a chair and complaining like a poor thing, while I continued with my part: "Well, see him there sitting there? Poor guy, he can't get up because of his rheumatism. I don't know how he even manages to sing with all that pain. The doctor said he should go to the mineral baths at Bitter Fountain, but of course he doesn't have the money. So me and his friends are trying to raise whatever we can – do you think you might make a contribution?"

"*Hombre*! Of course!"

The *señorito* called Antonio to tell him something, but to top it off, Antonio pretended to be deaf – the guy had to call him two or three times, and Antonio, with his hand cupped around his ear, got up with a cane, and me shouting: "Antonio, there is a *señor* here interested in helping you out with the baths at Bitter Fountain."

"God will repay you!" Antonio said, gratefully.

"No, *hombre*, it's nothing!"

He pulled out his wallet and gave him ten or twenty *duros*. Antonio kissed his hand with respect and I was busting up inside. Later when we were alone, we split the proceeds for the baths at Bitter Fountain.

Then another time: "Pericón, let's do the foot trick."

"What's the foot trick, Antonio?"

"Look, the foot trick is like this: when a *fiesta* is finishing up, we get a *señorito* to buy us a drink at the bar. When we're at the bar, you light up a cigarette, smoke awhile, and then throw it down. I go to stamp out the butt, but when I

151

step on it, I act like I've been burned; while I'm yelling, you tell him the story about my foot: 'Look, poor Antonio; he's so old that he has cracks on the bottom of his feet.' "

Of course, the *señorito* feels sorry for Antonio and gives him ten or twenty *duros* to buy some new shoes. Later we split and drink the proceeds, because Antonio el Mellizo was the most generous person I've known.

Once when we were finishing a *fiesta*, he said to me: "Pericón, tomorrow they're going to shut off my electricity."

"Really, Antonio?"

"I swear by my kids! Tomorrow they're shutting it off. But now let's go to the Vega bar and have some swordfish."

"But Antonio, what about the electricity?"

I didn't want him spending money on me, but there was no way to talk him out of it, because for him it was a joy to buy swordfish that they grilled for us and that we ate together – just the two of us in a room.

Enrique el Morcilla

Enrique el Morcilla was the best singer of *soleá* in all of Spain and the ugliest man in the entire world. When I sat and talked to Caracol's father about *cante*, I'd ask: "Who do you think is the best to have ever sung *soleá* in Spain?"

"The best to sing *soleá* is Enrique el Morcilla. But he looks like an animal. When he cries, the tip of his nose reaches his mouth, so he can lick the tears off, and he has a wart on the nape of his neck, sticking up, that looks like a half finger."

I remember, because of that wart, once, talking to Ignacio Espeleta about Enrique's *cante*, he said: "Oh – he's phenomenal! And furthermore, can he ever sleep. It's because the thing he's got on his neck isn't a wart at all – it's a screw. When he goes to bed, he loosens it, and removes his head, hangs it on the bedpost, and falls asleep ..."

But singing, he was the entire world – everything he sang he sang well. His *soleá* was to die, *siguiriyas*, to die, his father's *malagueña*, to die ... And the *media granaína* and everything – whatever he did, he'd put his stamp of the Mellizos on it.
Enrique sang three types of *soleá* from Cádiz that I always heard. First he'd come out with a short verse that said:

T'ahoga la vaniá.	You're drowning in vanity.
Y yo he visto una casa nueva	But I've seen a new house
derribarla un temporal.	brought down by a storm.

Then, the second verse:

Que venga el alba de veras.	Dawn is really coming.
A ver si viniendo el alba	Let's see if with the break of dawn
sosiega mi compañera.	my woman will rest.

And finally, he'd sing a double *cante* with the first line repeated:[65]

Le pío a Dios llorando,	I ask God, crying,
yo le pío a Dios llorando	I ask God, crying,
que me quite la salú	that he take away my health
y a ti te la vaya dando.	and give it to you.

Other times he'd sing different verses, but all in the style of Cádiz and Los Puertos, and all with that Mellizo stamp on them, that drove you crazy ... When he tried his hand at *siguiriyas*, you were out of your chair, the way he sang, with

---

[65] These three verses illustrate the structure of a performance of a *soleá cante*. The first verses tend to be shorter and understated, while the last verse is longer and delivered with more intensity. This last verse is sometimes referred to as "double" or "*macho*". In the case at hand, each verse is from the repertoire of *soleares* in the style associated with Cádiz, based on the styles developed by Enrique's father, Enrique el Mellizo.

that small little voice that went weaving and weaving with such an incredible sound ... On top of that, seeing how he looked, completely consumed, saying those *cantes*.   When he sang a verse from Loco Mateo, where he added three great *ay*'s, it was to die, with tears falling, him saying:

Yo firme t'he sío.	I've always been faithful.
Yo firme t'he sío.	I've always been faithful.
Y la curpita de que no te quiera	It's your fault that
tú l'habías tenío.	I don't love you.

My God! What went through your body!

But the poor guy couldn't hold his drink – with six drinks, he was wasted. He lost his strength and everything. With a lot of singers it's the opposite – the more they drink the better they are, but with him, if he drank too much – which always happened, because it didn't take much – he was useless, and tried to attack the *señoritos* if they didn't bring him more wine. Then he'd yell and scream: "*Olmol!!!*"

Because when he'd had enough wine, he wanted this *aguardiente* that they sold in Cádiz called *Olmo*. It was impossible to have him in a *fiesta*.   There was nothing to do but take him home. Weren't there ever times when I had to take him home drunk, yelling at me: "Pericón! *Olmol!*"

"All right, Enrique, when we get to the Mataero bar."

"No! *Olmol* – here!"

Any bar we passed, we had to stop there for his shot of *Olmo* – otherwise it was impossible to be with him. Of course, when a *Montañés* saw this ugly guy show up – and was he ever ugly, with those huge ears and his hat pushed back – screaming: "Olmol!"

The *Montañés* got scared and no *Olmo* nor nothing. Then Enrique yelled: "Vehicle!"

That meant he wanted a coach, because the poor guy couldn't walk anymore. The coach would come, we'd get in, and then on to the Mataero bar. He lived next door, but first he had to have his last shot of *Olmo*. Meanwhile, I called his nephew José, one of Antonio's sons. He came and got Enrique, who by this time couldn't even stand. He put him over his shoulder and took him upstairs to bed ...

But then three or four hours later, he'd be back in La Habana looking for me. I would get his money and keep it for him, for after he was sober. So he would show up and we'd go out to a fish fry place for a paper cone of fried fish. Then on a bench on Rosa Street we'd sit with our cone of fish, our plate of olives, our loaves of bread, and a half bottle of *valdepeñas*, all of that for six *reales*, back in those days. We stuffed ourselves and then argued about where to go – places where there would be *juergas*. We'd go to Tres Reyes or to the Kursal, or some other place ... In the Kursal, whenever Enrique showed up, there'd be a *fiesta*. And since he was so good to me, he'd plug for me to join.

I remember one night in the Kursal, around 4:30 in the morning; I hadn't earned a peseta and there was hardly anyone around. This guy came in alone and went straight upstairs to the gaming room. He'd been there a half hour when they started putting up tables, bottles of champagne, plates of everything – he'd ordered it all to have a *fiesta* with the bar girls that were there hanging out with us singers.

El Morcilla, el Troni, Capinetti, Aurelio, and me – we all joined the *fiesta*. You should have seen the *fiesta* – anything you wanted, you ordered it; the girls ordered whatever they wanted... It turned out the guy had broken the bank and had made a fortune. We were there until at least ten in the morning and, of course, el Morcilla tied one on with the champagne – everyone said: "Come on, Enrique, don't drink anymore."

"Leave me alone! Leave me alone! I've been here since 4:30 and I still haven't won anything!"

155

Don Antonio Chacón

One night in Villa Rosa about eight or ten artists were together in a *juerga*, when a *marqués* who was there sent for Chacón. He sent the message with a bootblack; when he came back: "Don Antonio says he can't come because he doesn't feel well." [66]

One of the artists blurted out: "Of course he's not coming – he knows we're all here."

With which he meant that he was intimidated by the artists there and was scared to come to the *juerga*. But a friend of Chacón's, who was there, heard this, got up and left, without saying anything. He found a card and wrote what had happened on the back. He then sent it to Chacón with the bootblack. When the bootblack arrived again at Chacón's house: "Didn't I tell you I couldn't come?"

"Excuse me, but they gave me this card."

Of course, when Chacón read it, he said: "Let's go."

They went to the Villa Rosa; as soon as the *Maitre d'* saw Chacón, he went running to tell them that don Antonio Chacón had arrived. He went to the room – all the other artists were terrified because they saw he'd come. Chacón, on the other hand, was calm; he sat down and ordered a half bottle of nectar – that was the wine he drank. They brought him the wine and he finished it off in three draughts. The other artists went on singing, while he sat next to the *marqués*, waiting. A half hour later, he ordered another half bottle, and polished it off in another three draughts, then he started feeling inspired.

---

[66] Antonio Chacón, although of humble origin, was so widely respected and comported himself in such a gentlemanly manner that he was referred to as 'don Antonio'. The title 'don', while now used almost universally, was then reserved for members of the aristocracy and elevated social classes.

He called Ramón Montoya, and seated him by his side, and he began to sing – and sing and sing; I don't know how long, but when he was done no one else dared to sing: "No – it's not my turn."

"But I already sang."

"Come on – it's your turn."

"But I sang before."

And those were the very best of Madrid in that room.

Even singing the way he did, he was a magnificent person – a gentleman who whatever he did, he did it sincerely, without cheating anyone. Another time, in a *fiesta* with the same *marqués*, when he finished singing the *marqués* got up and hugged him: "*Ole* Antonio! You are even better than Franconetti!"

"But what are you saying, *señor marqués*? Next to that giant I am but a little slipper!"[67]

But he was really a gentleman - he would always admit to anything anyone said to him. One night he was singing a verse while Arturo Pavón, Pastora, and Tomás' brother, were there. Arturo thought that Chacón sang it wrong. He told him, and instead of getting defensive, as people often do, Chacón said: "*Caramba*, Arturo, thanks so much for telling me; I've spent the last twenty years making a fool of myself with this verse, and until now, no one has said anything."

That's the way Chacón was.

I can't begin to tell you how he sang. The thing is that people who never heard him live will never know how this man sang. When he finally recorded he could barely walk and two guys had to carry him upstairs to the studio, because he couldn't support his own weight. So he wasn't even a shadow of what he was during his prime – the way I heard him in

---

[67] See Sevilla (2008) for a historical novel detailing Chacón's early dealings with Silverio Franconetti.

Cádiz.[68]

There once was a gentleman named Diego Mateo – a great *aficionado* – who would spend three or four days in a *juerga*, and loved Chacón with a passion. Once when he was in the Parra de la Bomba he decided to send for Chacón, sending a message to Madrid for him to come to Cádiz along with Ramón Montoya. This was in summer, in the month of August – all the best artist of Cádiz were there – el Morcilla, Antonio el Mellizo, el Troni, Antonia la Negra – a real black woman who sang and danced ... in other words, a great lineup of artists. Around ten at night a *Montañes* came and said that Chacón and Montoya had arrived from Madrid. Hugs, drinks – all the greeting stuff – and the *juerga* went on and on ... Around three in the morning, since it was so hot, they decided to move outside to some tables on the patio and continue the *fiesta*. Up until then, Chacón hadn't sung. A drink, then another, ... finally Diego Mateo said: "Well, don Antonio, could we hear you sing something?"

"Of course."

Montoya sat next to Chacón – at four in the morning, on a summer night, and he sang ...

Mother of my soul! That was insane! I remember that across the street from La Parra dela Bomba there was a building that took up the entire block, called "widow's house," because they never opened the windows. But that night, at four in the morning, with Chacón singing, the windows opened two by two, to listen to that man. I'll never forget.

---

[68] Pohren (1988:79) notes that Chacón resisted recording until, in his old age, financial pressures came into play. While contemporary accounts of Chacón's *cante* marvel at his vocal prowess, his recordings show him singing largely in a falsetto voice and are said to not be representative of his legendary *cante*.

Manuel Torre

I remember once when I was in San Fernando with Manuel Torre and Niño Gloria. When it was Manuel's turn to sing, I was sitting next to Gloria; he only started warming up with his *salida,* when the plaza seemed to shake and Gloria said to me: "*Ozú*, Pericón, he's pulled out the stops tonight."

He sang a *siguiriyas* that was frightening, it was so good. But no sooner had he finished, when some idiot said: "Manuel, *fandangos!*"

And that ruined everything. I don't know what he was thinking, but after having sung that *siguiriyas*, he didn't sing again. From there we went to Tres Reyes, with a guy named Camacho, who exported English roosters to Havana. We went into a room, and this guy sent for Aurelio and the Mellizos to fill out the *fiesta*. When it came time to order, Manuel felt like some tomatoes. So they had to find a platter of raw tomatoes to appease him. They brought him the tomatoes, he ate seven or eight of them with four or five shots of *aguardiente*, and came out singing in a way no one could touch – incredible! That sound of his got in your ear, and you couldn't forget it in three weeks. You had to humor Manuel in order to get him to sing with inspiration; you had to understand his genius and let him sing when he felt like it. You couldn't just say: "All right, Manuel, your turn to sing."

Because that way it was unlikely that he'd find his voice. Sánchez Mejías, who was a great and knowledgeable *aficionado*, never asked him to sing at a *fiesta*. When he arrived, he'd give him his *aguardiente*, or whatever he wanted, and let him have his space. The singing started – first this one, then the other, until finally, Manuel, dying to sing, said to Ignacio: "Igancio, are you going to let me sing?"

"Sure – if you want to."

And Manuel came out singing like a fury, eating up the

whole world.

There was a guy in Jerez who also understood him. Every time he brought him to sing, the first thing he'd do was give him a fighting cock that had won two or three fights. Of course, that put Manuel in a good mood, and that's when you had to hear him.

One year someone called him to sing *saetas* from his balcony. When word got around Jerez that Manuel Torre was going to sing *saetas* from this *señorito*'s balcony, the plaza was full of people waiting for the *saetas* a whole hour before the procession was due to arrive.

The Christ arrived, came near the balcony, and Manuel came out in his shirt sleeves – with the sleeves rolled up, with that that toupee over his forehead, and started singing *saetas*. Everyone was quiet, and when he was done and the procession had moved on, the *plaza* was littered with pieces of shirts and jackets, from the effect those *saetas* had.[69]

But then there were other times when he was horrible. Once they contracted him to sing for a week in Escudero Theater in Cádiz – it was across from Las Marinas bar in Plaza de las Flores. When people in Cádiz heard that Manuel Torre was singing, there was a huge to-do:

"Manuel Torre!"

"Manuel Torre is singing in the Escudero!"

"Manuel Torre is singing tomorrow!"

"Manuel Torre will be singing all week in Cádiz!"

"Manuel Torre ..."

The first night after selling out, he came and sang dreadfully. The next night only the real *aficionados* went again, and again, it was sold out, but Manuel was horrible. It went on like that for five nights – bad, bad, and worse, so of course, the

---

[69] This refers to the practice of tearing clothing during emotional moments (e.g. during weddings). There are several accounts of people ripping their clothes, while hearing Torre sing.

impresario called him and said: "Look Manuel, you've seen the theater full for five nights, but you also know that in these five nights you haven't sung the way you can, so if you don't mind, I'll pay you for the week, and you go now back to Sevilla. Because if this goes on for another two days, they'll tear the place down."

But Manuel would have none of it. He got headstrong and said he was contracted to sing for a week, and he would sing for a week. He went out again the sixth day – the same thing. But on the last day – the last day of the contract! – the night caught him, and did he ever sing! And after all that had happened, the owner wanted to renew his contract for another week. But Manuel said no – he was going to Sevilla, and he left for Sevilla the next day.

That's how he was all his life – the quirks of genius.

There was a time when he wasn't speaking to his godfather. One day his godfather was in a *fiesta* in the Pasaje del Duque with Antonio Chacón, Pastora, Tomás, ... in other words, the best of Sevilla. Manuel showed up, went to the bar, and ordered a shot of *aguardiente*. They told him who was upstairs – he ordered six or seven more shots, brought them upstairs, opened the doors to the room, and said to his godfather: "Godfather, excuse me, but could I sing something?"

Of course, his godfather loved him so much: "Whatever you like, Manolito."

And Manolito started in with *siguiriyas*, and left everyone shaking. Chacón put his face in the skirts of a girl there and couldn't stop crying. Another one the same, and another... When they finally came around, Manuel had jumped up and left – leaving them with the echo of his *siguiriyas*.

Tomás Pavón

One year, in the *feria de Sevilla*, Caracol's father called me to sing in a *caseta*; I went with Niño de Huelva and Tomás Pavón. Of course, the atmosphere in the *casetas* isn't conducive to *cante flamenco*, with all the noise and goings-on – particularly to sing serious things like *soleá* and *siguiriyas*. So when it was my turn, I came out with my *alegrías* and *bulerías* and let it all out. But I got scared just looking at Tomás' face, because in the *caseta* next door there was a piano that kept on playing *sevillanas*. One *sevillanas* after another. Poor Tomás – just thinking about having to sing with that piano next door made him ill, until the president of our *caseta* sent two or three messages next door, and finally got them to agree to stop the piano for a little while. That's when Tomás took advantage of the lull and sang a *siguiriyas*. After that, he didn't sing all night, because, of course, it was impossible.

Because of things like that they say he was very strange – this, that, and the other... But the thing about Tomás is that he was so serious about his *cante* and he knew that a lot of people who went to the theaters didn't understand or even like real *cante*. That's why he never sang in theaters; he had an artistic sensibility and knew that his *cante* was only for real *aficionados* who valued and understood what he did. Also, the way he sang required one to listen carefully and concentrate – something that is very hard where there are a lot of people. Then there were also *aficionados* who say he extended his *cante* too much. That's not true. It's one thing to extend and another to exalt. Extending is what some singers do, and they sound like they've fallen asleep singing. What Tomás did was to take a verse, and within the *compás*, add some tones and other things that drove you crazy listening to them. He was a giant!

Manolo Caracol

Once at the *feria de Sevilla* I decided to go to the Morillo bar, on Barca Street. When I got there, Caracol's father was there, and a little while later his son came with some *señoritos*. They went into a room for a *juerga* – first they sent for Caracol's father, then for me. I went in, sat, down, and proceeded to sing until seven in the morning. Caracol was drunk, I was drunk, and – well, the things that wine will do to you: one of the *señoritos*, who loved Caracol, gave him two bills every time he sang, but didn't give me anything – finally I said: "Hey – isn't there anything for me?"

He took it wrong, we argued, and he stormed off, leaving us alone – Caracol, me, and a guy from Cádiz called Lillo.

At that time in the morning, drunk on wine, Caracol got the idea of seeing his cousin, Rafael Ortega. We took a taxi to his house, and from there he sent for Manolo de Huelva. We drank a bottle, and another, and within a half hour, Manolo showed up. Guitar, singing, wine, and after two hours of *fiesta*, barely able to walk, we went to the Postigo bar on the Alemeda de Hércules and went into a room. Caracol ordered a bottle of wine – him paying, because when he had a few thousand *pesetas* in his pocket, they were already spent. I was singing *alegrías*, with Manolo de Huelva playing; singing and more singing until one time, Caracol, who had his head down on the table after throwing up all the wine he'd drunk, lifted his head and said: "Manuel, play *siguiriyas*."

De Huelva played and Caracol started in singing *siguiriyas* …

I swear by my children – may they die if it isn't true! I've never seen anything like it! I was crying like a baby, with my hair standing on end, listening to that man sing. How he sang – and after having drunk all that wine and throwing it up,

right there with his head between his legs.
May my children die, if it isn't true!

Aurelio Sellé

Nowadays, when people talk about Aurelio – people who have never heard him like I've heard them – right away they comment on this record, on that one... But they don't realize that Aurelio's recordings don't have anything to do with what he was able to do. When he first went to record, practically the entire record was stolen by Montoya, who only occasionally let Aurelio come in.[70] Then, when he went to record a second time, he wasn't in form and the record wasn't as it should have been.[71] But Aurelio, during his prime, was a world of *cante*, with that rough voice and that special style.

I remember one night I was at the Zapico bar on Rosa street, when don Manuel Camacho asked me: "Pericón, do you know where Aurelio and Capinetti hang out?"

"Yes sir."

"Well, go get them and come up to the room with them."

I went and found them and we went into the *fiesta*. There was don Manuel, a young woman, and Vicente Barrera, a kid of sixteen at the time – he'd come to fight the bulls at Puerto Santa María. Capinette took out the guitar, I sang – *alegrías*, *bulerías*, and *fandangos*... Finally, at three in the

---

[70] Traditionally, a guitarist's role is to accompany the singer, with a minimal amount of introductory material, etc. Ramón Montoya, perhaps because of his stature as a solo guitarist, may have played too long on his recording with Sellé. (See D-2, discography.)

[71] This second recording was made with Guitarist Andrés Herredia in 1962 (D-3).

morning – being in the summer, with the balconies open – don Manuel Camacho asked Aurelio: "Come on Aurelio, come on – I'd like Vicente to hear you sing."

Aurelio started in singing *soleá*, and it would be impossible to sing it with better timing – with that rough voice – it was scary. Then he sang *malagueñas* that couldn't be beat. But during one of the lulls, since it was so hot, don Manuel went out on the balcony to get some air and saw at least two hundred people standing on the sidewalk below, in ecstasy, listening to Aurelio sing. What a case!

Then there was also Chele Fateta, Aurelio's older brother, who took your breath away singing. But he was practically unknown because he didn't sing in public – you could give him anything in the world, but he lived from his work, when he could have lived from his *cante*. Everything he did and sang was phenomenal.

EPILOGUE: AFICIÓN AND *CANTE*

1.

*O*f course, nowadays there is a lot more *afición* than before. The thing is, before people had *juergas*, but not anymore. Now people will go to a *tablao* or some other place and don't have as many *juergas* as before. Those of us who had to live from *fiestas* know what it involves. We've experienced it all – the good, the bad, the real *aficionados*, and those who only wanted to party. Of course, we've had our share of the good and of the bad. Lots of times I'd see a party come into the Villa Rosa, go into a room, only to have to leave because the *fiesta* next door was so wild, you couldn't stand it. But then there were *señores* who showed up alone, only to listen to *cante*, without women or anything. They'd go into a room and spend ten to twelve hours just listening to *cante* – *cante*, wine, ham, fried fish ... I've seen it lots of times where a real *aficionado* would throw out women – beautiful women – but who wouldn't be quiet. The *señorito* would call the *Maître d'* and ask him to please escort the ladies out. On the other hand, others would show up with women and if someone asked them to be quiet, they'd tell him his job was to sing. Of course, there is no way to sing like that; they can give you all the money in the world and you can't sing. It's not about the money – they say they'll give you this and that – it's about how they treat you and their consideration and the respect they have for what you do. It's also how they attend to you – the little things: would you like a cigar? What kind of wine would you like? What would you like to drink? ... Then, even if you're hoarse, you'll still make the effort and come out singing.

But if they come out with *guasa* and aren't serious, you can't even open your mouth. If you have to, you do it with a bad attitude, and that's no way to sing, because you have to feel good to sing. Then there are the know-it-alls – the ones that don't know anything – nothing at all – but come impertinently asking for stuff, like the guy who told me that what I sang wasn't the real *malagueña*; the real one went "*qué bonitos ojos tienes debajo de esas cejas.*"[72] At that point, they can give you millions and you still won't sing. Or another guy one night in Cádiz asking for "black *bulerías*," and I had to sing seven or eight different kinds of *bulerías* until he finally said "that's it – those are the black *bulerías*." I can go on for three days about people like that: the tough guys, the dandies, the freeloaders ... And even though you've never had to say "yes" or "no" to anyone, you have to say "yes" to everything. If someone came in saying he had been so handsome, right off I'd loudly tell the guitarist that he must have had at least twelve or thirteen girlfriends when he was young. Hearing that, he'd give me a hug, and instead of twenty, he'd pay me forty. Or if some guy came in acting tough, I'd tell the guitarist how he had once kicked the crap out of four guys in Valencia, and of course, another hug and forty instead of twenty. The things I had to do in order to live from the *cante*; one always has to tell little lies in order to stay on good terms with the clients. Like the other day, when I was singing *soleá*: "What great *martinetes*, Pericón!"

Instead of saying "no – those weren't *martinetes*, they were *soleares*," I said "you really know a lot – because those were unusual *martinetes* that I sang with a *soleá* accompaniment." That way I made out and didn't lose the

---

[72] This *señorito* confused the Mexican song *Malagueña Salarosa* (popularized by the Trio group, Las Calaveras), with the flamenco *malagueña* Pericón sang.

client.

I remember during the contest for *alegrías* in Cádiz, when Manolo Vargas won first prize and I won second,[73] we went to an after-party with some of the judges, and one of the judges – one of the judges! – after I'd been singing *soleá,* came and hugged me: "Pericón – those *malagueñas! Ole!*"

There's nothing to do but continue on with your own art. But the worst were the freeloaders. These are the ones that come to the *fiestas* with the *señoritos,* and don't spend a *duro.* They eat, drink, and listen to this one and the other one's *cante,* but since they've ingratiated themselves to the one paying you, you have to kiss up to them, knowing you won't get a *duro* out of them. They're just there freeloading and you have to be nice to them, put on a face, while inside ...

Then singing in a theater, it's pretty much the same. If you have a good audience, you'll feel like singing, and you'll eat up the house. But if you come on scared and see something odd in the first row, you'll be off kilter and not on your toes. It's that the *cante* is so delicate that any little thing can influence whether you're in form or not: how the people are listening, if they're attentive, if they spur you on. If they listen with respect and later talk to you with respect, without pretending to know everything, in those occasions, you've found real *afición* and that's when you really sing well.

2.

Cante flamenco is the only thing on planet Earth that, if you learn it without *compás,* you sing well, but still can't sing because you lack the most important thing – which is the *compás.* It's like writing well but not knowing how to spell. That's the way it is with those who don't know *compás;* they

---

[73] This would be the 1952 *Concurso de Alegrías*; see the appendices under Manolo Vargas.

might sing well, but they don't know how to sing, because they are lacking in the fundamental: *compás*. Because, of course, every *cante* has its meter. If you don't know how to measure it, then nothing – you'll never say anything. There are singers who sing well and have pretty voices, and everything, but don't reach you because they don't measure the *cante*. On the other hand, there are others with practically no voice at all, but who use it measuring out the *cante* well, and you say how good it is. You also have to know how to match the *cante*'s *compás* with the guitar's *compás*, so that the two are on the same road at the same time. Otherwise, it is impossible, and instead of *cante flamenco*, it sounds like a catfight. Then there are the voices – there are pretty voices, but when it comes time to sing *soleá* or *siguiriyas*, they're not so pretty. These cantes require voices that are profound – voices that have *eco* and leave their *eco* embedded in your body. Finally, there is *afición*. If you don't have *afición*, you have no business in flamenco. *Afición* requires you to be a slave and a martyr to the trade – always thinking how to sing better, to learn more, to know more, and to do it better. Even Ramón Montoya – and I'm saying Ramón Montoya – when we were at the Villa Rosa, he'd practice through dinner, letting it get cold. Even with him being a monster guitarist, he practiced and practiced. The same thing as with the guitar goes for the *cante*, and goes for everything. If you have no *afición*, you'll never amount to anything.

Appendices

People

Disclaimer: Birth and death dates of flamenco artists, particularly from before the 20ᵗʰ century, are notoriously inaccurate. Therefore, the dates cited here should be taken as approximate. I have flagged a few dates that are particularly suspect.

Almadén, Jacinto   Francisco Antolín Gallego (1905-1968). "El Niño de Almadén", following Antonio Chacón, specialized in *cante andaluz*, particularly *cantes del Levante*. He was also known for his interpretation of *tientos*.

La Argentinita   Encarnación López Júlvez (1898-1945). Born in Argentina of Spanish parents and raised in Northern Spain, La Argentinita was a major pioneer in theatrical flamenco/Spanish dance during the first part of the 20th century.

Aurelio de Cádiz   See Aurelio Sellé.

de Badajoz, Manolo Manuel Álvarez Sorubet (1889-1962). One of the most recorded accompanists during the second quarter of the 20th century. He was house guitarist for the Regal label, and therefore, accompanied the greatest singers of the time. He had a very flamenco, albeit choppy, approach to the guitar.

El Camarón de la Isla José Monje Cruz, (1950-1992). The most influential singer of the late 20th century. Born in La Isla de San Fernando, near Cádiz, he moved to Madrid, where he collaborated with guitarist Paco de Lucía, producing a modern style of flamenco which, while rooted in traditional flamenco, made flamenco relevant to the younger generation. Camarón had and has a quasi-cult following, both among young *Gitanos* and Spanish intellectuals. A statue in his honor is in front of La Venta de Vargas in San Fernando.

Canalejas de Puerto Real   Juan Pérez Sánchez (1905-1966). A very popular singer of *fandangos* and *bulerías* during the 1930s.

Capinetti, José   José Capinetti Rodríguez. A prominent guitarist of the Cádiz scene, but less-known elsewhere. He was a favorite guitarist of Aurelio Sellé. According to Blas Vega (1978:15), after attending Campinetti's funeral around 1950, Pericón went straight from the cemetery to the train station and moved to Madrid. See Part 2, "Capinetti".

Caracol, Manolo   Manuel Ortega Juárez (1909-1973). A major singer of the 20th century. He sang traditional flamenco in a very *Gitano* manner, but also sang numerous *zambras* and *cuplés* with orchestra, often with Lola Flores. He appeared in a number of Spanish and Mexican movies. He opened Los Canasteros, long one of the top *tablaos* in Madrid. His statue stands in the Alemeda de Hércules, Sevilla, He made numerous recordings, including a two-LP anthology of *cante flamenco* (D-4). He was killed in a car accident in 1973. See Part 5, "Manolo Caracol".

Chacón, Antonio   Antonio Chacón García (1869-1929). A Jerez-born non-*Gitano* singer who was perhaps the most influential singer of the late 19th century and a principle innovator of *cante andaluz*. He is credited with creating several important *cantes*, including styles of *malagueña*, and *granadinas*. Sevilla (2008) is a historical novel that chronicles Chacón's early life. Blas Vega (1990) is the definitive biography. See Part 5, "Antonio Chacón".

Chele Fateta   José Sellés Nondedeu (1860-1913).

Older brother of Aurelio Sellés. Noted as a great interpreter of *cante jondo*, but shunned professional activity in flamenco.

Chiclanita, José José María Salrio Gómez (1874-1957?). Cádiz –based singer who bridged the 19th and 20th centuries and remembered long-forgotten *cantes*. According to Pohren (1988:76), he died in the 1940s in his eighties, although Lafuente (1955), writing about the early 1950s, describes him then as an octogenarian. See Part 2, "Chiclanita".

Cojo Peroche Antonio Vargas Gómez ('The Cripple Peroche'). Brother of Manuel Vargas, Cojo Peroche was a famous *festero* and humorous character in Cádiz. There is one commercial recording of him, originally a cut on his brother's LP (D-14), where he sings various *bulerías*, each verse more off-key than the last, and ending in an excruciating rendition of *Cielito Lindo*; rumor has it that the musicians (Paco de Lucía, Manolo Sanclúcar, and Felipe Campuzano) purposely set the key too high. There are numerous stories about his witty one-liners.

Durán, Rosita Rosa López Caballero (b. 1922-1999). Jerez-born dancer, whose career was associated with La Zambra.

Espeleta, Ignacio (1871-1938). A colorful character and influential singer during the early 20th century. He is credited, perhaps apocryphally, with creating the "*tiri-ti-tran" salida* to *alegrías* during a production of "*Las Calles de Cádiz*" (see Part 1, "*Las Calles de Cádiz*"), when he was allegedly drunk and couldn't remember the words. Poet García Lorca mentions him in his lecture on *cante jondo* ("There stood Ignacio Espeleta, handsome as a Roman turtle, who was asked once why he never worked, replied with a smile worthy of

Argantonio: 'How am I to work if I come from
Cádiz?'") See Part 2, "Ignacio Ezpeleta".
El Feo de Cádiz   Juan Fernández Fernández ('the ugly
one from Cádiz'). Macandé's older brother; he worked
as a dancer in Argentina from about 1915 until 1930.
Flores, Lola   María de los Dolores Flores Ruiz (1923-
1995). Jerez-born singer/dancer/actress who, although
not a *Gitana*, grew up in the *Gitano* neighborhood of
San Miguel, Jerez (where a statue in stands in her
honor). She was known for her popular flamencoized
songs, as well as for playing the fiery Gypsy in
numerous films. She was also Manolo Caracol's long-
time artistic partner – her dances to his *zambras* are
still imitated today. Throughout her life she was a
regular feature in Spanish tabloids. Thousands attended
her funeral.
Franconetti, Silverio   Silverio Franconetti Aguilar (1829-
1889). One of the most influential singers of the 19th
century. His influence was enhanced by his role as a
flamenco *impresario*, as he was co-owner of Sevilla's
Café Burrero, and later opened Café Silverio, two of the
most famous *café cantantes*. His career in Spain was
interrupted by a ten-year hiatus when he fled to
America after allegedly killing another singer. See
Sevilla (2008).
el Gallo, Rafael   Rafael Gómez Ortega (1882-1960).
Famous bullfighter from the early 20th century. Known
for his unusual antics (e.g. fighting from a chair) and
humor. A member of the flamenco/bullfighting Ortega
family, he was married to flamenco dancer Pastora
Imperio.
Gandulla, Juan   See Habichuela.
Gardner, Ava   Ava Lavinia Gardner (1922-1990).
American film star who spent considerable time in

Spain and frequented the Madrid *tablao* La Zambra. Once married to Frank Sinatra, she was known for her numerous loves and heavy drinking.

Gloria, El Niño   Rafael Ramos Atúnez (1893-1954). *Gitano* singer from Jerez, noted for his creations in *fandangos* and *bulerías*. He was also renowned for his interpretations of *saetas* and *villancicos*. His artistic name comes from a *villancico* with *"gloria"* in the chorus.

Habichuela   Juan Gandulla (1860-1935). A Cádiz guitarist and a student of *el Maestro* Patiño (unrelated to the Habichuela guitarists from Granada). He can be heard on a few early 20th Century recordings with Antonio Chacón.

de Huelva, Manolo   Manuel Gómez Vélez (1892-1976) - also known as "el Niño de Huelva". A major and very influential guitarist of the first half of the 20th century, he was rather secretive of his playing and often refused to play, or played in a limited capacity, if there were other guitarists present. Because of this, the few recordings he made do not reveal the guitarist that he was.

Jumán   Juan Martínez Neto (1925-1993). Pericón's oldest son, a noted photo journalist for the *Diario de Cádiz*.

Lobato, Chano   Juan Miguel Ramírez Sarabia (1927-2009). A non-*Gitano* singer   from barrio de Santa María. He was known as one of the last singers in the vein of Pericón. Like Pericón, he was a noted story-teller. His statue stands outside the Centro de Arte Flamenco La Merced

de los Lobitos, Bernardo   Bernardo José Álvarez Pérez (1886-1969). Singer from Alcalá (Sevilla), he was known as a great interpreter of *cante andaluz*, particularly less-known rural cantes, such as *trilleras* and *nanas*.

Loco Mateo   Mateo Lasera (1832-1890). A singer, born in Ronda, but associated with Jerez, where he lived most of his life. He was an influential singer of *soleares* and *siguiriyas*. He is reputed to have been instrumental in the development of *bulerías*. According to Pohern (1988: 48) he suffered from mental illness, as his nickname would suggest. However, others (e.g. the Flamenco World biography, https://www.flamenco-world.com/tienda/autor/loco-mateo/57/) suggest his nickname was due to his great sensitivity, where he would sometimes break into tears while singing.

López, Pilar   (1912 - or 1906-2008). La Argentinita's sister, a major figure in theatrical dance companies during the 20th century.

de Lucía, Paco   Francisco Sánchez Gómez (b. 1947). The most influential guitarist in modern times. He revolutionized the flamenco guitar in the late 20th century. Known for impeccable technique and perfect timing, he became flamenco's top soloist as well as the usual accompanist for much of Camarón's career. Later, he experimented with a jazz quintet format and ushered in the era of *flamenco nuevo*.

el del Lunar, Perico Pedro del Valle Pichardo (1894-1964). A renowned accompanist with an encyclopedic knowledge of *cante*. He was instrumental in putting together the first flamenco anthology in 1954 (D-5), for which he allegedly taught some of the singers lesser-known cantes. He was a long time fixture at Madrid's La Zambra (see Part 1, "From Zambra to the World"). His son, Perico el del Lunar, Hijo, carried on in his father's tradition, continuing at La Zambra.

Macandé   Fernando Gabriel Fernández Fernández (1897-

177

1947). *Gitano* singer born in the barrio de la Viña, but later moved to Botica Street, in barrio de Santa María (where there is now a commemorative plaque). He was known for his interpretation of *siguiriyas* and for suffering from mental illness; indeed, his nickname is a Gypsy word for 'crazy'. See Cobo Guzmán (1977) for a biography and Part 2, "Macandé".

La Macarrona Juana Vargas (1860-1947). One of the great dancers of the late 19th century.

Maestre, Polciano The last Civil Governor of Cádiz during the Monarchy of Alfonso XIII; he was replaced with the declaration of the Second Republic in April, 1931.

Mairena, Antonio Antonio Cruz García (1909-1983). One of the most influential singers of the mid-20th century. A *Gitano* from Dos Hermanas (Sevilla), he was instrumental in the resurgence of *cante gitano* in the 1950s and 1960s. He directed an important anthology in 1965 (D-1) and recorded a three-LP anthology in 1966 (D-11). His book, co-authored with poet Ricardo Molina (Molina and Mairena 1963), was one of the first comprehensive descriptions and histories of *cante flamenco*.

Manolete Manuel Laureano Rodríguez Sánchez (1917-1947). Considered by many to be the greatest bullfighter of all times. Famous for his minimalist approach, where he would remain stationary for several passes. His death in the bullring was followed by three days of official mourning.

de Marchena, Melchor Melchor Jimémez Torres (1907-1980). *Gitano* guitarist from Marchena (Sevilla), he was one of the finest accompanists of the 20th century.

Marchena, Pepe José Tejada Martín (1903-1976). Perhaps the most popular singer of the early 20th century. While he had a good knowledge of *cante* *flamenco*, he concentrated on rather commercialized *cante andaluz*, and was a leading exponent of the *ópera flamenca* movement. Born in Marchena (Sevilla). See Part 1, "On tour with Marchena".

el de la Matrona, Pepe   José Núñez Meléndez (1887-1980). Encyclopedic singer, born in Sevilla, but spent most of his career in Madrid. He favored *cante jondo*, specializing in obscure forms. His 1970 anthology (D-12) received the Premio Nacional del Disco de la Cátedra de Flamencología. His stories were collected in a companion book to this one in Ortiz Nuevo (1975).

el Mellizo, Antonio   Francisco Antonio Jiménez Espeleta (1874-1936). One of Enrique el Mellizo's sons. A singer in Cádiz' *fiesta* scene, he helped maintain his father's school of *cante*. See Part 5, "Antonio el Mellizo".

el Mellizo, Enrique   Francisco Antonio Enrique Jimènez Fernández (1848-1906). A *Gitano* singer from the barrio de Santa María. Considered the father of the Cádiz school of *cante*. He created styles of *soleá*, *siguiriyas*, and *malagueña*, and may have been instrumental in the creation of *tientos and alegrías*. His *malagueña* is said to contain influences of Gregorian chant. While he sang semi-professionally, he worked in the slaughterhouse and was a *puntiello* in *matador* Manuel Hermosilla's *cuadrilla*. See Part 5, "Enrique el Mellizo" and del Río Moreno (no date) for a biography.

Menese, José   José Menese Scott. (1942-). Born in La Puebla de Cazalla (Sevilla), a non-*Gitano* who nevertheless specializes in *cante gitano*.

Mojama, Juanito   Juan Valencia Carpio (1892-1957). A Jerez-born *Gitano* whose career was largely in the *fiesta* scene in Madrid. Known for his *bulerias* and *Gitano* delivery.

Montoya, Jarrito   Roque Montoya Herredia (1925-1995). From San Roque (Cádiz). A singer with wide knowledge of *cante flamenco*, who performed in numerous theatrical companies and films.

Montoya, Ramón   Ramón Montoya Salazar (1880-1949). One of flamenco's most influential guitarists. Along with Niño Ricardo, Montoya defined the modern flamenco guitar. He made the first recording of flamenco guitar solos in 1926.

el Morcilla, Enrique   José Enrique Jiménez Espeleta (1877-1929). Another of Enrique el Mellizo's sons. Morcilla is short for Hermosilla, after *matador* Manuel Hermosilla – Enrique's brother's godfather. The nickname may also be a joke: *morcilla* means 'blood sausage,' while *hermoso* means 'handsome'. As Pericón notes, Enrique was known to be particularly homely. Enrique carried on the tradition of his father's *cante* and created his own style of *soleá*. See Part 5, "Enrique el Morcilla".

Morente, Enrique   Enrique Morente Cotelo (1942-2010). Born in Granada, Morente learned his *cante* in Madrid from Pepe de la Matrona. As a result, he had an encyclopedic knowledge of *cante flamenco*. Nevertheless, he was one of flamenco's most influential innovators, experimenting with new sounds, often involving drawn-out melodic lines, particularly in *cantes del Levante* and slow *tangos*. He has also made a number of influential fusion recordings. On the other hand, he has recorded traditional *cante*, including a two volume tribute to the *cante* of Antonio Chacón (D-13), for which he won the Spanish Ministry of Culture's first prize for popular music – the first flamenco recording to be so honored. His daughter, Estrella Morente, is a leading flamenco/flamenco-fusion singer.

La Niña de los Peines See Pastora Pavón.

el Nitri, Tomás   Tomás de Vargas Suárez Ortega de la
Cera (1850-188?). A *Gitano* singer from Puerto de
Santa María, known for his *siguiriyas*. He was awarded
the first *Llave de Oro de Cante Flamenco* ('Golden
Key' – an unofficial highest honor).

Ortega Family   A *Gitano* dynasty of bullfighters and
flamenco artists, long associated with Cádiz, the most
famous being singer Manolo Caracol (son of Manuel
Ortega, el del Bulto) and bullfighter Rafael el Gallo.
See Pohren (1988:149) for a family tree.

Ortega, Rafael   (early XX century-1973). A Sevilla-born
dancer, long associated with Pilar López and known for
his wit. He was featured in a few Mexican Cine de Oro
productions with singer-dancer Lola Flores. A member
of the Ortega dynasty, he was first cousin to Manuel
Ortega el del Bulto and Rafael el Gallo.

La Papera, Rosa   Non-professional *Gitana* singer from the
barrio de Santa María (where there is now a street
named after her). She is credited with creations in
bulerías and *cantiñas*, but best known as the mother of
La Perla de Cádiz. Her nickname comes from the fact
that she sold fried potatoes (*papas*) on the street. See
Part 2, "Rosa la Papera".

La Pasionaria   Dolores Ibárruri Gómez (1895-1989).
Left-wing activist who served in the Spanish Parliament
during the Second Republic and, many years later, in
the post-Franco democracy. Famous for the Civil War
slogan *¡No pasarán!* 'They won't pass!', she served as
president of the Spanish Communist Party in exile, and
then in Spain after Franco.

Patiño, el Maestro   José Patiño González (1829-1902).
Gitano guitarist from the barrio de Santa María. He
was one of the earliest guitarist on record and a major

accompanist in the *café cantante* scene from mid-19th century Sevilla. After retiring, he taught guitar in Cádiz; a good deal of the standard flamenco guitar repertoire might be traced to him.

Pavón, Arturo   Arturo Pavón Cruz (1880-1959). Older brother of Pastora and Tomás Pavón. Reputed to have a vast knowledge of *cante*, but without the vocal facilities of his siblings.

Pavón, Pastora   Pastora María Pavón Cruz (1890-1969). Also known as La Niña de los Peines. A *Gitana* from Sevilla, she was perhaps the greatest woman singer during the first half of the 20th century. She was known as a *festera*, specializing in *tangos* and *bulerías*, but sang *cante jondo* as well. She was the sister of Tomás Pavón and was married to Pepe Pinto.

Pavón, Tomás   Tomás Pavón Cruz (1893-1952). A *Gitano* singer from Sevilla and an important singer of *cante jondo*. He was the brother of Pastora Pavón. See Part 5, "Tomás Pavón".

La Perla de Cádiz   Antonia Gilabert Vargas (1925-1975). *Gitana* singer from the barrio de Santa María and daughter of Rosa la Papera. She was known as a *festera*, singing distinctive *bulerías*, *cantiñas*, and *tangos* (perhaps based on her mother's *cantes*). Her *cante* had a major influence on Camaron de la Isla. The old slaughterhouse, adjacent to barrio de Santa María, has been converted into a *peña* in her honor. Her statue stands outside the *peña* and there is a street named for her in the barrio de Santa María.

Pinto, Pepe   José Torres Garzón (1903-1969). Singer in the *ópera flamenca* tradition, but an admirer of *cante gitano* – particularly that of his wife, Pastora Pavón, and his brother-in-law, Tomás Pavón.

Piquer, Conchita   Concepción Piquer López (1908-1990).

Actress and *cuplé* singer (*coplista*).
El Pollo   Manuel Pérez. A student of el Maestro
Patiño and favorite guitarist of Enrique el Mellizo.
Ricardo, Niño   Manuel Serrapí Sánchez (1904-1974).
Sevilla-born guitarist who, while a sought-after
accompanist, was one of the most influential flamenco
guitar soloists. He was a major influence on Paco de
Lucía's guitar playing.
Romero, Rafael   Rafael Romero Romero (1910-1991).
Gitano singer born in Andújar (Jaen), Romero worked
in paid *fiestas* until he was contracted at the Madrid
tablao La Zambra in the 1950s.
Sánchez Mejías, Ignacio (1891-1934). A famous bullfighter
during the early 20th century, his death in the bullring
was the subject poet García Lorca's *Lamento por
Ignacio Sánchez Mejías*. He was associated with the
Generation of '27 intellectual movement (which
included García Lorca and Manuel de Falla), and was a
patron of the arts. In the context of flamenco, in
addition to sponsoring the theater production "*Las
Calles de Cádiz*" (see Part 1, "*Las Calles de Cádiz*", he
was romantically involved with La Argentinita at the
time), he put on numerous paid *fiestas*.
Sellé, Aurelio   Aurelio Sellés Nomdedeu (1887-1974).
A non-*Gitano* singer from the barrio de Santa María, he
was an important link between the *cante* of Enrique el
Mellizo and later *cante* in Cádiz. He played an
instrumental role in defining the Cádiz style of *cante*.
See del Río Moreno (2001) for a biography and Blas
Vega (1978) for an extensive interview. There is a
street named for him in central Cádiz, and a plaque in
his honor in the house where he was born in barrio de
Santa María. See Part 5, "Aurelio Sellé".
Tío de la Tiza   Antonio Rodríguez Martínez (1833-

1911). Perhaps the most famous *murgista* from the
Cádiz Carnival. There is a *plaza* named for him in the
barrio de la Viña He is best known for composing the
Duros Antiguos ('Old Coins') *tanguillo*, which spoofs
the clamor that ensued when, in 1904, Mexican treasure
washed up on the beach. This *tanguillo* remains the
unofficial anthem of Cádiz. His nick-name 'chalk guy'
comes from the fact he worked in a tavern, where he
kept the tabs written on the bar in chalk. See Moreno
Criado (1980) for a biography.

Torre, Manuel   Manuel Soto Loreto (1878-1933). A
Jerez born *Gitano*, who was a major figure in the
flamenco ambience during the early 20th century. He is
considered the most moving singer of *siguiriyas* in
history. See Part 5, "Manuel Torre".

Valderrama, Juanito   Juan Valderrama Blanca (1916-
2004). A very popular singer in the *ópera flamenca*
style, whose career extended into the 21st century.

Varea, Juan   Juan Varea Segura (1908-1985).
Madrid-born singer who worked in touring groups
during the *ópera flamenca* period and then sang for the
large *cuadro* in La Zambra.

Vargas, Manolo   Manuel Vargas Gómez (1907-1970). A
Cádiz-born singer from a family of *Gitano* flamenco
singers. He represented the typical *cantes* from Cádiz,
winning first prize for *alegrías* in the 1952 National
Contest (Pericón won second prize); several
performances from that contest were recorded and
released on D-6. Manolo Vargas sang in La Zambra
and ran a fried fish store in Madrid's working-class
Vallejas neighborhood. A plaque in his honor is on the
house where he lived in Cádiz, on Libertad Street.

Las Viejas Ricas   'The Old Rich Ladies'. One of the most
famous *chirigotas* of the late 19th century Carnival. As

their name suggests, they dressed up as old rich ladies.

El Vivillo   Joaquín Camargo Gómez (1865-1929).
One of the last of Spain's famous highway robbers
(*bandoleros*). As *bandoleros* were defeated by the
Guardia Civil in the early 20th century, El Vivillo
escaped to Argentina, but was subsequently extradited
to Spain in 1909, where he was eventually acquitted of
all charges. He became a romanticized media persona
in Madrid, but ended up committing suicide. See Part
2, "El Vivillo" and his autobiography (Camargo Gomez
1981).

Glossary and Places

El 606 A bar on Rosa Street; there is a current bar on the same street with the same name, but is not the same as the flamenco bar from these stories.

afición Enthusiasm; a deep interest in something. In this context it means a deep interest in flamenco. Someone with *afición* is an *aficionado*.

Aguaducho A bar on Sacramento Street near San Rafael; it was later renamed Petit Kursaal.

aguardiente 'Fire water' – any type of clear distilled liquor.

aire Air, feeling.

alegrías A festive *cante chico* in the major key with a 12-beat rhythm. This is the prototypical *cante* from Cádiz.

Alemeda de Hércules A street in Sevilla – an important center of flamenco activity during the early 20th century.

ángel 'angel' – a type of humor similar to *gracia*, but with the connotation of a good-natured personality.

arsa A term of encouragement, similar to *ole*.

asturianas A *cante* based on a song form from Asturias.

bandarillas Large darts with colored paper, used to wound the bull in a bullfight. The person who inserts the *banderillas* is a *banderillero*.

baile Flamenco dancing.

bicho Often means 'bug', but can refer to any despised animal, similar to 'varmint'.

bulerías A driving festive 12-beat *cante chico* that is ubiquitous in flamenco *fiestas*. The style of *bulerías* sung in Cádiz tends to be light and witty, often in the major key.

Café Borrull This must refer to the Villa Rosa in Barcelona,

which was one of the most important centers of the
Barcelona scene. It was owned by the Borrull family,
which included guitarists Miguel Borrull, father and
son.

café cantante A type of flamenco venue from the mid to late
19th century.

cagón   Someone who craps a lot.

Caleta   A beach/fishing harbor on the Atlantic side of
Cádiz, next to the barrio de la Viña. Since this beach is
so emblematic of Cádiz, *Caletero* is applied to someone
steeped in the ambience of Cádiz.

Las Calles de Cádiz An innovative theater production which
simulated the flamenco ambience of Cádiz. It was
originally produced by La Argentinita. According to
Pohren (1988, p. 226), she was aided and inspired for
this production by her lover, the famous bullfighter
Ignacio Sánchez Mejías. The production began in 1933
and was redone in 1940 under the direction of Conchita
Piquer. The artists, who included dancers brought out
of retirement (La Macarrona, La Malena, and La
Sordita), as well as Pericón, El Niño Gloria, and
Ignacio Espeleta, acted out street scenes in Cádiz'
barrio de Santa María. The artists played roles of
neighborhood characters such as the shoemaker, the
policeman, etc. See Part 1, *"Las Calles de Cádiz"* and
Part 2 " Ignacio Ezpeleta".

Campo del sur The road that runs along the southern,
Atlantic side of Cádiz.

canino   Starving, hard-up – it suggests a desperate,
canine hunger, and brings up the image of a skeletal
scavenging street dog. The general term for 'hunger' of
this type is *canina*.

cante Flamenco singing. *Cante chico* forms are light styles,
while the deepest, most melancholy forms are referred

to as *cante jondo*. *Cante gitano* refers to style most closely associated with *Gitanos*, while *cante andaluz* refers to those associated with non-*Gitanos* (*Payos*). Many *cante andaluz* forms are also *cante libre* – that is, they have no fixed *compás*. *Cante flamenco* is flamenco singing in general.

cantes del Levante   *Cantes* from the mining regions in eastern Andalucía, including *tarantas, mineras*, and *cartegeneras*.

cantiñas   A *cante* similar to *alegrías*. It is also used to refer to the family of *alegrías*-like *cantes* (e.g. *caracoles, romeras, mirabrás*).

la caña   A *cante-jondo* form similar to *soleá*. It may be similar to an older *cante* that evolved into *soleá*.

Capuchinos   A plaza on Atlantic side of Cádiz, on Campo del sur and the site of a Capuchin monastery. There was a psychiatric hospital there until about the 1970s. This is the hospital where singer Macandé ended up and where Enrique del Mellizo sang for the inmates (see Part 2, "Macandé" and Part 5, "Enrique el Mellizo".).

caracoles   A *cante* similar to *alegrías*, but with a distinctive melody.

cartegenera   A *cante del Levante* form, based on eastern Andalucian *fandangos*, and associated with Cartegena. The guitar accompaniment is usually in F#, with open strings, that result in a type of discord characteristic of the *cantes del Levante*.

Casablanca   A *venta* past Puerta Tierra, near the beach.

caseta   A temporary structure put up in *ferias*; some are open to the public and may serve food and drink and offer entertainment; others are private.

céntimo   1/100th of a *peseta*.

chirigota   A costumed singing group that sings satirical songs during Carnival.

compás   Rhythm, particularly flamenco rhythm.

Corona   A *venta* outside Puerta Tierra; see Part 4,
"Pericón thief!".

Cruz Verde A small *plaza* in the Callejones area of Cádiz,
near the barrio de la Viña. This is the epicenter of the
Cádiz Carnival.

cuadrilla   The bull fight retinue associated with a *matador*,
including *banderilleros* (who wound the bull with large
darts – *banderillas)*, *picadores* (who wound the bull
with from horseback with lances), and the *puntillero*
(who kills the bull by severing the spinal chord with a
knife, after the *matador* has disabled it).

cuadro   A flamenco ensemble.

cuplé   Spanish popular songs. There is a tradition of
performing these with flamenco (guitar) or with a
typically Spanish orchestral accompaniment. While
many Spaniards are ambivalent towards pure flamenco,
culpés enjoy great popularity. A singer of *culpés* is
called a *cupleista*.

disparate   Something unexpected.

duende   'spirit' – the inexplicable catharsis that can
accompany a particularly moving flamenco
performance. This term is used more often by
intellectuals than by flamenco artists themselves,
perhaps due to Federico García Lorca's famous lecture
La Teoria y Juego del Duende ('The theory and
function of *duende*').

duro   A coin worth five *pesetas*; until the Euro was
introduced in 2002, prices were often quoted in *duros*.

eco   'echo' – this refers to a certain voice quality that
is particularly well-suited to *cante jondo* forms like
siguiriyas.

Eureka   A chain of bread dispensaries.

Falange   The fascist political party founded by José Antonio Primo de Rivera in 1933. Its doctrines were largely adopted by the Franco government after the Spanish Civil War. The Civil War (1936-1939) came about when Franco and three other generals led a coup attempt against the Second Spanish Republic. The post-war period was particularly difficult, as these stories suggest. Spain remained a dictatorship until Franco's death in 1975.

fandangos   A flamenco form that is based on a common type of Andalucian folk music. Most often it refers to a *cante libre* that retains melodic elements from folkloric *fandangos*, but by dispensing with the rhythm, allows the singer to draw out the notes and use it as a vocal show piece. Also called *fandanguillos*.

feria de Sevilla Sevilla is famous for its Spring fair, which takes place two weeks after Holy Week. Originally a regional livestock fair, this has evolved into a week-long party. The fairgrounds are lined with *casetas* – make-shift structures, that house both private and public parties. Major flamenco artists were regularly contracted to work in these *casetas*, but many *casetas* play non-stop *sevillanas* and other types of popular music.

festero   A singer who specializes in festive *cantes* such as *bulerías* and *tango,* and is generally humorous.

fiesta   'party' – in this context a flamenco party, usually with flamenco artists hired by *señoritos*.

flamenco nuevo A genre of modern flamenco characterized by jazz-influenced tonality and the use of instruments not traditional in flamenco. The term is used for music styles that range from fusion music by major Spanish flamenco artists, to flamenco-flavored New Age/Smooth Jazz music produced outside of Spain by

Gabi	musicians with little flamenco training. I have not found anyone who remembers what this is. From the context, it appears to be a type of canned food used in field rations that came with red powder (perhaps for coloring?). *Gabi* must be a brand name, long forgotten.
Gaditano	Someone from Cádiz (from the Roman name *Gades*).
Gallego	Someone from Galicia; a large number of *Gallegos* immigrated to Cádiz, where they had a reputation for their business acumen (also see *Montañese* and Part 2 "*Gallegos* and *Montañeses*").
Gitano	Spanish Roma (Gypsy).
gracia	Humor – Cádiz is famous for its *gracia*.
granaína	A *cante libre* developed by Antonio Chacón, based on the local *fandangos* associated with the Granada region.
guajiras	A major key *cante* in 12 beats, based on Cuban music.
guasa	A type of wise-ass humor that often has a mean edge to it.
La Habana	A flamenco bar on Rosa Street.
Jerez de la Frontera	A town about 25 miles inland from Cádiz. It is famous for its sherry wine production, its horses, and bulls. In the present context, it is significant for producing scores of the very best *Gitano* performers throughout the history of flamenco. See Zatania (2007) for the role of agricultural labor around Jerez in the development of flamenco in the region.
juerga	A party, with connotations of debauchery. In this context, it is a synonym for a flamenco *fiesta*.
(barrio de) La Libertad	Neighborhood in central Cádiz near the public market and the post office (Plaza de la Flores).

levante   An easterly wind. It blows hot in the summer and cold in the winter. It is supposed to put people's nerves on edge.

libre   Free. In the context of *cante*, this refers to forms with no fixed rhythm (*cante libre*). Most *cante andaluz* forms are *libre*.

malagueña   A *libre cante andaluz* form developed in the late 19th century from the folkloric dances around Málaga. Antonio Chacón and Enrique el Mellizo were both renown for their malagueña creations. In Cádiz, the *malagueña del Mellizo* is part of the local canon of *cante*. It is common to warm up for the *malagueña del Mellizo* with a *granaína* verse (or a *media granaína* under the older nomenclature), These flamenco *malagueñas* are unrelated to the piano piece (often played on guitar) by the Cuban composer Ernest Lecuona (although it is clear he modeled this piece on the general chord structure of flamenco *malagueñas*).

maricón   A Gay man; the term is derogatory, but ubiquitous.

martinete   A very intense *cante jondo* form that is sung without guitar accompaniment. From *martillo* 'hammer', it is associated with blacksmiths.

matador   The star bullfighter, who tires the bull with passes and cape work. After suffering wounds from the *banderilleros* and the *picadores*, the bull is disabled by the *matador*'s sword. The bull is then quickly killed by the *puntillero*.

matarife   The one who kills livestock in a slaughterhouse. Since *matarifes* knew how to slaughter the animal quickly, they often worked as *puntilleros* in bullfights.

media botellita A half bottle of sherry.

media granaína A *libre cante* originally sung as a warm up to the *granaína*. Interestingly, the nomenclature has switched: what was once called *media granaína* is now called *granaína*, and vice versa (see Navarro García 1993: 185-188).

Medina Sidonia A town in the hills above Cádiz, founded by the Phoenicians; it may be actually older than Cádiz itself. It is one of the more important ducal seats in Spain and is noted for its pottery.

(barrio del) Mentidero A neighborhood in Cádiz in the northern part of the old city. The name is based on the word *mentir* 'to lie', and refers to a gathering place for gossip.

milonga A flamencoized song form, originally from Argentina. While initially sung to a *rumba*-like rhythm, it evolved into a *libre* staple of the *ópera flamenca* repertoire.

minera A *cante del Levante* form, based on eastern Andalucian *fandangos*. The guitar accompaniment is usually in F#, with open strings, the result being a type of discord characteristic of the *cantes del Levante*. When played as a guitar solo (and sometimes in accompaniment), it is played in A-flat, following Ramón Montoya. The verses deal with mining themes.

mirabrás A *cante* similar to *alegrías*, but with a distinctive melody.

Montañese Someone from the "Mountain" – i.e. Santander and the surrounding northern region of Cantabria. A large number of *Montañeses* immigrated to Cádiz, where they had a reputation for their business acumen; the term can also be used for 'small grocery store' (also see *Gallego* and Part 2 "*Gallegos* and *Montañeses*").

murga A an older term for *chirigota*; a *murgista* is a member of a *murga*.

mus A card game similar to bridge.

nana A flamenco lullaby.

ole   The standard term of encouragement;
sometimes the accent is on the final syllable ('olé').

ópera flamenca A genre of flamenco *cante* that began around
1910 and continued into the 1950s. This movement de-
emphasized *cante gitano*, and presented a rather
saccharine variety of flamenco that had great popular
appeal.

ozú   An interjection; short for 'Jesús'.

palmas   The rhythmic hand claps that accompany
flamenco. Often one or more keep the basic rhythm,
while others clap between the beats; the result is quite
impressive.

peña   A social club ,where members and others gather
around a theme – e.g. flamenco, bullfighting, Carnival,
football, etc. Often they are named after their founder
or after a respected artist, There are currently many
flamenco-themed *peñas* in each major town or city in
Andalucia (as well as in Madrid and elsewhere). Some
of them are responsible for sponsoring flamenco
festivals.

perra chica/gorda Two small denomination coins were the
perra chica 'little dog' and the *perra gorda* 'fat dog';
their value was 5 and 10 céntimos respectively (1
peseta = 100 *céntimos*). They were so named because
it was thought that the lion on the coat of arms looked
more like a dog.

peseta   The standard monetary unit in Spain from 1859
until it adopted the Euro in 2002. In the 1970s-2000, a
peseta was roughly equivalent to a US penny.

peteneras   A *cante* in 12 beats and in the minor key that is
reputed to bring bad luck (based on an incident where a
dancer died after performing it). Many artists,
including many *Gitanos*, refuse to perform or listen to
it. Nevertheless, many others, including *Gitanos* Rafael

Romero and El Camarón de la Isla, have recorded versions of it.

Petit Kursaal   A bar on Sacramento Street near San Rafael, formerly Aguaducho.

picador   Part of the *cuadrilla* in a bullfight. The *picador* is on horseback from where he stabs the bull with a lance.

Piñata Sunday   The first Sunday of Lent and the last day of Carnival.

Plaza de la Catedral The plaza in front of the Cádiz cathedral.

Plaza de las Flores   A plaza in central Cádiz in the barrio de La Libertad, adjoining the public market and home of the post office. It is named after the flower stands that occupy one end of the plaza.

Plaza San Juan de Dios   A large plaza near the harbor and the barrio de Santa María; location of the City Hall.

pregón   A street vendor's song.

pringá   Cheap cuts of fatty meats typically used in a variety of Andalusian stews (*pucheros*).

La Privadilla A bar/restaurant on Gaspar del Pino Street. Due to its proximity to the Oratorio de San Felipe Neri, where Spain's first liberal constitution was signed in 1812, it was a center of political discussion during the early 19th century.

Puerta Tierra   'Land-side Gate' – the entrance to the old city of Cádiz. Beyond Puerta Tierra is a narrow peninsula,that eventually becomes the causeway that connects Cádiz, which is virtually an island, to San Fernando. In Pericón's time the area outside Puerta Tierra would have been semi-rural. Today it is the site of the new city of Cádiz, which is larger than the old city.

Puerto Real   A town on the mainland, across the bay from Cádiz. Since 1969 it has been connected to Cádiz by a

195

bridge (Puente de Caranza); during the time period in
the story, Pericón would have had to take the train
through San Fernando, circling the Bay of Cádiz.

Puerto Santa María Another town across the bay from Cádiz
– north of Puerto Real. A ferry service connects it with
Cádiz; currently a new bridge connecting Puerto Santa
María to Cádiz is under construction.

Los Puertos A place name that designates the port towns
across the bay from Cádiz, including Puerto Real and
Puerto Santa María.

puntillero The member of a bullfighting team (*cuadrilla*)
who kills the bull with a short knife to the spinal chord
after the *matador* disables it.

pupilero A tour guide who specialized is taking tourists
to brothels and connecting them with flamenco artists.
See Part 2, "Bars and brothels".

real A coin worth a quarter of a *peseta* – in years
past, prices were often quoted in *reales*.

romera A *cante* similar to *alegrías*, but with a
distinctive melody.

Rota A town on the Atlantic, north of Puerto Santa
María. A US NATO base was built there in the 1950s.
A ferry service connects Rota with Cádiz.

rumba An upbeat song form in 4/4 time, imported into
flamenco from Cuba.

saetas 'darts'. Songs sung to images of the Virgin or
Christ during Holy Week. Mounted on floats in the
Holy Week procession, these images pass down the
streets, stopping so that the bearers can rest. During
these rests, *saetas* are sung, often from balconies.
Primitive *saetas* may have been precursors to some of
the *cante jondo* forms of *cante flamenco*.

salida An introductory warm up before singing the first
verse of a *cante*.

San Fernando La Isla de San Fernando is an island in the salt
marshes south of Cádiz, connected by a causeway.
Historically known as La Isla de León, it was the scene
of a battle during the Napoleonic War and was the
birthplace of El Camarón de la Isla.

Sanlúcar de Barrameda A town on the Atlantic coast, at the
mouth of the Gaudalquiver river, north of Rota.

San Severiano An area south of Puerta Tierra, where the army
had a munitions deposit that exploded on August 18,
1947, perhaps due to a defective land mine.
Approximately 150 people died in the explosion and
5000 were wounded.

Santa Catalina   A 16th century fortress near the Caleta
beach, on the Atlantic side of Cádiz. It was used as a
prison, particularly for prominent prisoners, from the
19th century until 1991. Today it hosts art exhibitions
and theater events.

(barrio de) Santa María   A neighborhood of Cádiz in the
southwestern part of the city, near the southern city
gates (Puerta Tierra). It is Cádiz' oldest neighborhood
and historically home to much of the *Gitano*
population. It was adjacent to the bullring and the
slaughterhouse, where many *Gitanos* worked. The
bullring is gone and the slaughterhouse has been
converted into a *flamenco peña* in honor of La Perla de
Cádiz. Several famous singers, including Enrique el
Mellizo and Aurelio Sellé, were born there.

seguiriya   One of the deepest of the *cante jondo/cante
gitano* forms. Its rhythm is in 12s, but with a different
cycle than most other 12-beat forms.

señoritos   Rich men who hired artists for a party; the term
can be used pejoratively.

sereno   'night watchman' – they wore uniforms, were
armed with nightsticks, and had the keys to all the

buildings on their beat. Upon arriving home, without a key, a hand-clap would alert the *sereno* to open the door, for a tip. The tradition died out in the 1970s.

serrana   A rural *cante* associated with the mountainous region of Andalucia. It has a rhythm similar to *siguiriyas*, but is slower and more solemn.

sevillanas   A folkloric music and dance form, tangentially related to flamenco. It is a particular version of the widespread *seguidillas*, a dance form in 3/4 time found throughout central and southern Spain (other *seguidillas* include *seguidillas manchegas*, from La Mancha and *panaderos*). *Sevillanas* are danced in couples to either live or recorded music and are ubiquitous during the *feria de Sevilla.*

soleá/soleares A *cante jondo/cante gitano* form with a 12-beat rhythm; one of the most common flamenco song forms.

tablao   A type of flamenco nightclub that began in the 1950s. These became a major force in the commercialization of flamenco, which played an important role in marketing Spain as a tourist destination in the 1960s. Nevertheless, *tablaos*, while presenting commercial flamenco, often employed major artists and often offered some of the best professional flamenco available.

tango   A festive *cante chico* in 4/4 time. Unrelated to the Argentinean *tango*.

tanguillo   A song form in 6/8 time that is sung during Carnival.

tapas   Small portions of food traditionally given gratis with a drink. Nowadays there is usually a charge for *tapas* in Cádiz.

taranta   A c*ante del Levante* form, based on eastern Andalucian *fandangos*. The guitar accompaniment is usually in F#, with open strings, that result in a type of

discord characteristic of the *cantes del Levante.* Often
the verses deal with mining themes.

tientos A cante similar to *tango,* but performed more
slowly, hence, approaching *cante jondo.* Often
accompanied with a slow syncopated ('dotted') rhythm.

Tres Reyes A bar at the end of the Plaza de las Viudas, near
Via Murguía.

trillera A rural *cante* associated with wheat harvests.

Turisbar A bar that was near Puerta Tierra.

valdepeñas A variety of wine (usually red) produced in the
Valdepeñas region (southern Castile).

venta A roadside inn/tavern. These were outside city
limits and remained open as truck stops. When bars
were forced to close early, flamenco *fiestas* often
moved to these *ventas.*

villancico A Christmas song.

Villa Rosa One of the major centers of flamenco in Madrid
in the 1950s. It survived as a *tablao* into the 1980s.
Noted for its tile work (a historical landmark), it still
stands at the corner of the Plaza de Santa Ana. It has
recently re-opened as a *tabalo.*

(barrio de la) Viña A neighborhood in the western,
Atlantic side of Cádiz, near the Caleta beach/fishing
harbor. Originally the site of a vineyard, it became a
fishermen's neighborhood. While many flamenco
artists come from La Viña, it is more closely tied to
Carnival. As Pericón's son told me: "Santa María is
more flamenco, but La Viña is more g*aditano.*"
Pericón, while in Cádiz, lived in La Viña for most of his
adult life.

Vito's A *venta*/restaurant beyond Puerta Tierra; the
scene of Pericon's famous "Smokey" story; see Part 4,
"Pericón, Thief!".

zambomba   An instrument played during Christmas Eve celebrations. It is made from a ceramic pot with a pig skin and a pole and resembles a butter churn. The player slides his or her hand over the pole, creating vibrations on the skin, making a very distinctive sound.

zambra   A *cante*, similar to *tango*, with a distinctive Middle-Eastern sound. Manolo Caracol popularized a type of commercial *zambra* that was sung with an orchestral accompaniment.

La Zambra   The first *tablao* to open in Madrid (1954).

Discography

D-1 *Antología del cante flamenco y cante gitano.* Decca, 258.031-32-33, 1965.

D-2 Aurelio de Cádiz. *Arte Flamenco, vol 4. El Cante de Antaño.* Mandala MAN 4840. CD reissued from slate 78s recorded by Polydor in 1929.

D-3 *Aurelio Sellés, el de Cádiz.* Hispavox HH10-194, 1962.

D-4 Caracol, Manolo. *Una historia del cante flamenco.* Hispavox, HH 10-23/24, 1958.

D-5 *Cante flamenco: Anthology.* Westminster, WL-5304, 1954.

D- 6 *De Cádiz ... aquella Venta de Vargas, Cultura Jonda 4.* Fonomusic, M-26811-97, 1997.

D-7 de Cádiz, Pericón. *Cantes de Cádiz.* Clave, 18-1216 (S), 1971.

D-8 de Cádiz, Pericón. *Cantaores Gaditanos, Vol. 5.* Clave, 1973.

D-9 Lobato, Chano. *Azucar candé.* Palo Nuevo, 2000.

D-10 *Magna antologia del cante flamenco.* Hispavox, S/C 66-201, 1982.

D-11 Mairena, Antonio. *La gran historia del cante gitano-andaluz.* Colombia, MCE 814/816, 1966.

D-12 el de la Matrona, Pepe. *Tesoros del flamenco antiguo.* Hispavox, HH 1-346/47, 1970.

D-13 Morente, Enrique. *Homenaje a Don Antonio Chacón.* Hispavox, HH 7243 8 37653, 1977.

D-14 Vargas, Manolo y Cojo Peroche. *Cantaores Gaditanos, Vol 4.* Clave, D/FLA-077, 1973.

References

Blas Vega, José. 1978. *Conversaciones flamencas con Aurelio de Cádiz.* Librería Valle, Madrid.

Blas Vega, José. 1990. *Vida y cante de Don Antonio Chacón: La edad de oro del flamenco* (1869-1929). Cinterco, Madrid.

Camargo Gómez, Joaquín (alias Vivillo). 1981. *Memorias del Vivillo.* Libreria Renacimiento, Sevilla.

Cobo Guzmán, Eugenio. 1977. *Pasión y Muerte de Gabriel Macandé.* Colección El Duende 4. Ediciones Demófilo, Madrid

del Río Moreno, Francisco. 2001. *Aurelio Sellé: Cantándole a Dios.* Cátera Itinerante de Flamencología, Cádiz.

del Río Moreno, Francisco. no date. *El Mellizo en el Cádiz de su tiemo (1848-1906).* Librería Raimundo, Cádiz.

Lafuente, Rafael. 1955. *Los Gitanos, el flamenco, y los flamencos.* Editorial Barna, Barcelona.

Mintz, Jerome R. 1997. *Carnival song and society : gossip, sexuality, and creativity in Andalusia.* Berg, Oxford and New York.

Mitchell, Timothy. 1994. *Flamenco: Deep Song.* Yale University Press, New Haven.

Molina, Ricardo and Antonio Mairena. 1963. *Mundo y formas del cante flamenco.* Revista de Occidente, Madrid.

Moreno Criado, Ricardo. 1980. *Antonio Rodríguez: El Tío de la Tiza, su vida y su obra.* Ediciones Jiménez-Mena, Cádiz.

Navarro García, José Luis. 1993. *Cantes y bailes de Granada.* Editorial Arguval, Málaga.

Ortiz Nueve, José Luis. 1975. *Recuerdos de un cantaor sevillano: Pepe de la Matrona.* Demófilo, Madrid.

Peralta, Belén, 2009. *Recorrido sentimental por la ciudad de Cádiz*. Ediciones Absalon, Cádiz.

Pohren, D. E. 1988. *Lives and Legends of Flamenco: A Biographical History*. Society of Spanish Studies, Madrid.

Sevilla, Paco. 2008. *Seeking Silverio: the Birth of Flamenco*. Sevilla Press, San Diego.

Solís, Ramón. 1988. *Coros y chirigotas: Carnaval en Cádiz*. Silex, Madrid.

Zatania, Estela. 2007. *Flamencos de Gañanía: Una mirada al flamenco en los cortijos históricos del bajo Guadalquivir*. Ediciones Giralda, Sevilla.

About the Author

Flamencologist José Luis Ortiz Nuevo has served as director of the *Bienal de Flamenco de Sevilla* for fifteen years and is currently Advisor to the Museum of Dance "Cristina Hoyos".

About the Translator

John Moore is a professor of linguistics at the University of California at San Diego. He is also a   long-time flamenco *aficionado* and has led groups of students to explore Spanish culture and subcultures, including flamenco, in study abroad programs.